**TEACHER'S PET PUBLICATIONS**

PUZZLE PACK
for
1984
based on the book by
George Orwell

Written by
William T. Collins

© 2005 Teacher's Pet Publications
All Rights Reserved

The materials in this packet are copyrighted
by Teacher's Pet Publications, Inc.

These pages may be duplicated by the purchaser
for use in the purchaser's own classroom.

Copying any of these materials and distributing them
for any other purpose is a violation of the copyright laws.

© 2005 Teacher's Pet Publications
www.tpet.com

INTRODUCTION
If you already own the LitPlan for this title, this Puzzle Pack will refresh your Unit Resource Materials and Vocabulary Resource Materials sections plus give you additional materials you can substitute into the tests. If you do not already have a complete LitPlan, these pages will give you some supplemental materials to use with your own plan. There are two main groups of materials: one set for unit words (such as characters' names, symbols, places, etc.) and one set for vocabulary words associated with the book.

WORD LIST
There is a word list for both the unit words and the vocabulary words. These lists show you which words are being used in the materials and the clues or definitions being used for those words. You may want to give students a word list with clues/definitions to help them, or you may want students to only have a word list (without clues/definitions) if you want them to work a little harder. Both are available for duplication. The word lists can also be your "calling key" for the bingo games.

FILL IN THE BLANK AND MATCHING
There are 4 each of the fill in the blank and matching worksheets for both the unit and vocabulary words. These pages can be used either as extra worksheets for students or as objective parts of a unit test. They can be done individually if students need extra help or as a whole class activity to review the material covered.

MAGIC SQUARES
The magic squares not only reinforce the material covered but also work on reasoning and math skills. Many teachers have told us that their students really enjoy doing these!

WORD SEARCH PUZZLES
The word search words go in all directions, as indicated on your answer keys. Two of the word search puzzles have the clues listed rather than the words. This makes the puzzle a little more difficult, but it reinforces the material better. Two word search puzzles have words only for students who find the clue puzzles too difficult.

CROSSWORD PUZZLES
Both unit and vocabulary word sections have 4 crossword puzzles.

BINGO CARDS
There are 32 individual bingo cards for the unit words and 32 individual bingo cards for the vocabulary words. You can use your word list as a "call list," calling the words at random and marking them off of your list as you go, or you could use the flash cards by cutting them apart and drawing the words at random from a hat (or box or whatever). To make a better review, you might ask for the definition and spelling of each word as you call it out–or you could call out the definitions and have students tell you the words they need to look for on the puzzle.

JUGGLE LETTERS
The vocabulary juggle letter game is intended to help students learn the spellings of the words. One sheet has the definitions listed on it as an extra help for students who need it or to reinforce the definitions if you choose to do so.

FLASH CARDS
We've included a set of vocabulary flash cards you can duplicate, cut, and fold for your students. Some teachers make a few sets for general use by the class; others make a set for each student. Some teachers duplicate them for each student and have the students cut & fold their own. You can cut out just the words and put them in a hat, have each student pick out one word and write the definition and a sentence for that word. Students then swap words and papers, with the next student adding a sentence of his own under the last one. You can have students swap as many times as you like. Each time the student will read the sentences written prior to his own and then add a sentence. You can cut out the words and definitions separately and play "I Have; Who Has?" Each student in the room draws a word and definition. The first student says, "I have (the name of the word). Who has the definition?" The student with the definition reads it then says, "I have (the name of the vocabulary word she has). Who has the definition?" The round continues until all words and definitions have been given.

1984 Word List   **1984**

No.	Word	Clue/Definition
1.	AMPLEFORTH	Sent to Ministry of Love for leaving the word God in a verse
2.	ANTIQUE	Winston and Julia meet in its upstairs room; ___ shop
3.	ATOMIC	Real concept from the 1960's connected to the novel; ___ war
4.	BOOK	Contains the history of the Party & the Brotherhood; The ___
5.	BROTHER	Head of the Party; Big ___
6.	BROTHERHOOD	Conspirator group against the Party: The ___
7.	CHARRINGTON	Runs the antique shop; really a member of the Thought Police
8.	CHILDREN	Taught at school to spy on parents & others
9.	DESPAIR	Mood of the novel
10.	DIARY	April 4, 1984 is the day Winston starts his ___
11.	DIVORCE	Not allowed by the Party
12.	DOUBLETHINK	Having two contradictory thoughts at the same time
13.	DOWN	Winston's diary entry: ___ with Big Brother
14.	DUCKSPEAK	Speech that sounds like the quacking of a duck
15.	EASTASIA	Enemy superstate in the middle of the novel
16.	EURASIA	Enemy superstate as novel opens
17.	FACECRIME	Having the wrong look on one's features
18.	GOLDSTEIN	Enemy of the People; image used to create hatred; Emmanuel ___
19.	HATE	Group frenzy agains the Brotherhood; Two Minutes ___
20.	INGSOC	English socialism; philosophy of the Party
21.	JULIA	Hates the Party but participates enthusiastically
22.	LONDON	Setting of the novel
23.	LOVE	Maintains law and order; Ministry of ___
24.	MINILUV	Ministry of Love in Newspeak
25.	MINIPAX	Ministry of Peace in Newspeak
26.	MINIPLENTY	Ministry of Plenty in Newspeak
27.	MINITRUE	Ministry of Truth in Newspeak
28.	NEWSPEAK	Language that narrows the range of thought
29.	OBRIEN	Re-educated Winston; wrote part of The Book
30.	OCEANIA	Superstate ruled by the Party
31.	OLDSPEAK	Language that is gradually being replaced
32.	ORWELL	Author of 1984
33.	PAPERWEIGHT	Winston bought it; it is destroyed when he is captured
34.	PARSONS	He is denounced by his daughter
35.	PEACE	Responsible for war related events; Ministry of ___
36.	PLENTY	Responsible for economic affairs; Ministry of ___
37.	POLITICAL	B vocabulary consists of words used for ___ purposes
38.	POWER	Ultimate goal of the Party
39.	PROLES	Only hope for revolution may be with them
40.	RATS	Winston's main fear and eventually his breaking point
41.	REINTEGRATION	Learning, understanding, acceptance are ___ stages
42.	SCIENCE	Newspeak has no word for this concept
43.	SENSE	Common ___ was the heresy of heresies
44.	SLAVERY	Freedom is ___
45.	SLOGAN	War is peace is a Party ___
46.	SMITH	Rewriting and distorting history was ___'s job
47.	STRENGTH	Ignorance is ___
48.	SYME	Writing the 11th Edition of the Newspeak dictionary is ___'s job
49.	TECHNICAL	C vocabulary consists of words used in ___ fields
50.	TELESCREEN	Two-way image and sound observation device
51.	THOUGHT	___ Police observe and arrest people for crimes

No.	Word	Clue/Definition
52.	THOUGHTCRIME	Thinking that is not allowed
53.	TORTURED	O'Brien _____ Winston until he believed 2+2=5
54.	TRUE	Winston knew 2+2=4 was ____
55.	TRUTH	Responsible for news, entertainment, education, arts; Ministry of ___
56.	WAR	Aim is to use products but not raise standard of living
57.	WATCHING	Big Brother is _____ you
58.	WINSTON	He doesn't believe in the Party doctrine
59.	WORDS	A vocabulary consists of everyday ____

1984 UNIT FILL-IN-THE BLANK 1

_____   1. Winston knew 2+2=4 was ____

_____   2. Having the wrong look on one's features

_____   3. Sent to Ministry of Love for leaving the word God in a verse

_____   4. Contains the history of the Party & the Brotherhood; The ___

_____   5. He doesn't believe in the Party doctrine

_____   6. Language that is gradually being replaced

_____   7. Big Brother is _____ you

_____   8. Enemy superstate in the middle of the novel

_____   9. Ministry of Peace in Newspeak

_____   10. Thinking that is not allowed

_____   11. Ministry of Plenty in Newspeak

_____   12. Head of the Party; Big ___

_____   13. Responsible for economic affairs; Ministry of ___

_____   14. Group frenzy agains the Brotherhood; Two Minutes ____

_____   15. B vocabulary consists of words used for ____ purposes

_____   16. Winston and Julia meet in its upstairs room; ___ shop

_____   17. April 4, 1984 is the day Winston starts his ___

_____   18. Responsible for war related events; Ministry of ___

_____   19. War is peace is a Party ____

_____   20. Superstate ruled by the Party

1984 UNIT FILL-IN-THE BLANK 1 KEY

TRUE	1. Winston knew 2+2=4 was ____
FACECRIME	2. Having the wrong look on one's features
AMPLEFORTH	3. Sent to Ministry of Love for leaving the word God in a verse
BOOK	4. Contains the history of the Party & the Brotherhood; The ____
WINSTON	5. He doesn't believe in the Party doctrine
OLDSPEAK	6. Language that is gradually being replaced
WATCHING	7. Big Brother is ____ you
EASTASIA	8. Enemy superstate in the middle of the novel
MINIPAX	9. Ministry of Peace in Newspeak
THOUGHTCRIME	10. Thinking that is not allowed
MINIPLENTY	11. Ministry of Plenty in Newspeak
BROTHER	12. Head of the Party; Big ____
PLENTY	13. Responsible for economic affairs; Ministry of ____
HATE	14. Group frenzy agains the Brotherhood; Two Minutes ____
POLITICAL	15. B vocabulary consists of words used for ____ purposes
ANTIQUE	16. Winston and Julia meet in its upstairs room; ____ shop
DIARY	17. April 4, 1984 is the day Winston starts his ____
PEACE	18. Responsible for war related events; Ministry of ____
SLOGAN	19. War is peace is a Party ____
OCEANIA	20. Superstate ruled by the Party

1984 UNIT FILL-IN-THE BLANK 2

_____	1. Setting of the novel
_____	2. April 4, 1984 is the day Winston starts his ___
_____	3. Winston's main fear and eventually his breaking point
_____	4. Taught at school to spy on parents & others
_____	5. Enemy of the People; image used to create hatred; Emmanuel ___
_____	6. Responsible for war related events; Ministry of ___
_____	7. Common ___ was the heresy of heresies
_____	8. Rewriting and distorting history was ___'s job
_____	9. Aim is to use products but not raise standard of living
_____	10. Conspirator group against the Party: The ___
_____	11. Enemy superstate in the middle of the novel
_____	12. War is peace is a Party ___
_____	13. Responsible for economic affairs; Ministry of ___
_____	14. Language that narrows the range of thought
_____	15. Enemy superstate as novel opens
_____	16. Learning, understanding, acceptance are ___ stages
_____	17. Ministry of Love in Newspeak
_____	18. A vocabulary consists of everyday ___
_____	19. C vocabulary consists of words used in ___ fields
_____	20. Contains the history of the Party & the Brotherhood; The ___

1984 UNIT FILL-IN-THE BLANK 2 KEY

LONDON	1. Setting of the novel
DIARY	2. April 4, 1984 is the day Winston starts his ___
RATS	3. Winston's main fear and eventually his breaking point
CHILDREN	4. Taught at school to spy on parents & others
GOLDSTEIN	5. Enemy of the People; image used to create hatred; Emmanuel ___
PEACE	6. Responsible for war related events; Ministry of ___
SENSE	7. Common ___ was the heresy of heresies
SMITH	8. Rewriting and distorting history was ___'s job
WAR	9. Aim is to use products but not raise standard of living
BROTHERHOOD	10. Conspirator group against the Party: The ___
EASTASIA	11. Enemy superstate in the middle of the novel
SLOGAN	12. War is peace is a Party ___
PLENTY	13. Responsible for economic affairs; Ministry of ___
NEWSPEAK	14. Language that narrows the range of thought
EURASIA	15. Enemy superstate as novel opens
REINTEGRATION	16. Learning, understanding, acceptance are ___ stages
MINILUV	17. Ministry of Love in Newspeak
WORDS	18. A vocabulary consists of everyday ___
TECHNICAL	19. C vocabulary consists of words used in ___ fields
BOOK	20. Contains the history of the Party & the Brotherhood; The ___

1984 UNIT FILL-IN-THE BLANK 3

_____ 1. Two-way image and sound observation device

_____ 2. English socialism; philosophy of the Party

_____ 3. Winston's main fear and eventually his breaking point

_____ 4. War is peace is a Party ____

_____ 5. Speech that sounds like the quacking of a duck

_____ 6. Writing the 11th Edition of the Newspeak dictionary is____'s job

_____ 7. Maintains law and order; Ministry of ___

_____ 8. O'Brien _____ Winston until he believed 2+2=5

_____ 9. Rewriting and distorting history was ___'s job

_____ 10. Winston knew 2+2=4 was ____

_____ 11. He is denounced by his daughter

_____ 12. Winston's diary entry: ___ with Big Brother

_____ 13. Winston and Julia meet in its upstairs room; ___ shop

_____ 14. Freedom is ___

_____ 15. Superstate ruled by the Party

_____ 16. Contains the history of the Party & the Brotherhood; The ___

_____ 17. C vocabulary consists of words used in ____ fields

_____ 18. Aim is to use products but not raise standard of living

_____ 19. Ignorance is ___

_____ 20. Enemy of the People; image used to create hatred; Emmanuel ___

1984 UNIT FILL-IN-THE BLANK 3 KEY

TELESCREEN	1. Two-way image and sound observation device
INGSOC	2. English socialism; philosophy of the Party
RATS	3. Winston's main fear and eventually his breaking point
SLOGAN	4. War is peace is a Party ____
DUCKSPEAK	5. Speech that sounds like the quacking of a duck
SYME	6. Writing the 11th Edition of the Newspeak dictionary is ____'s job
LOVE	7. Maintains law and order; Ministry of ___
TORTURED	8. O'Brien ____ Winston until he believed 2+2=5
SMITH	9. Rewriting and distorting history was ___'s job
TRUE	10. Winston knew 2+2=4 was ____
PARSONS	11. He is denounced by his daughter
DOWN	12. Winston's diary entry: ___ with Big Brother
ANTIQUE	13. Winston and Julia meet in its upstairs room; ___ shop
SLAVERY	14. Freedom is ___
OCEANIA	15. Superstate ruled by the Party
BOOK	16. Contains the history of the Party & the Brotherhood; The ___
TECHNICAL	17. C vocabulary consists of words used in ____ fields
WAR	18. Aim is to use products but not raise standard of living
STRENGTH	19. Ignorance is ___
GOLDSTEIN	20. Enemy of the People; image used to create hatred; Emmanuel ___

1984 UNIT FILL-IN-THE BLANK 4

_____ 1. Real concept from the 1960's connected to the novel; ___ war

_____ 2. Winston and Julia meet in its upstairs room; ___ shop

_____ 3. Big Brother is _____ you

_____ 4. Sent to Ministry of Love for leaving the word God in a verse

_____ 5. Learning, understanding, acceptance are ___ stages

_____ 6. Ministry of Truth in Newspeak

_____ 7. Two-way image and sound observation device

_____ 8. Having two contradictory thoughts at the same time

_____ 9. Having the wrong look on one's features

_____ 10. He is denounced by his daughter

_____ 11. Responsible for war related events; Ministry of ___

_____ 12. Thinking that is not allowed

_____ 13. Hates the Party but participates enthusiastically

_____ 14. O'Brien _____ Winston until he believed 2+2=5

_____ 15. Ultimate goal of the Party

_____ 16. April 4, 1984 is the day Winston starts his ___

_____ 17. Winston knew 2+2=4 was _____

_____ 18. Aim is to use products but not raise standard of living

_____ 19. B vocabulary consists of words used for _____ purposes

_____ 20. Runs the antique shop; really a member of the Thought Police

1984 UNIT FILL-IN-THE BLANK 4 KEY

ATOMIC	1. Real concept from the 1960's connected to the novel; ___ war
ANTIQUE	2. Winston and Julia meet in its upstairs room; ___ shop
WATCHING	3. Big Brother is _____ you
AMPLEFORTH	4. Sent to Ministry of Love for leaving the word God in a verse
REINTEGRATION	5. Learning, understanding, acceptance are ___ stages
MINITRUE	6. Ministry of Truth in Newspeak
TELESCREEN	7. Two-way image and sound observation device
DOUBLETHINK	8. Having two contradictory thoughts at the same time
FACECRIME	9. Having the wrong look on one's features
PARSONS	10. He is denounced by his daughter
PEACE	11. Responsible for war related events; Ministry of ___
THOUGHTCRIME	12. Thinking that is not allowed
JULIA	13. Hates the Party but participates enthusiastically
TORTURED	14. O'Brien _____ Winston until he believed 2+2=5
POWER	15. Ultimate goal of the Party
DIARY	16. April 4, 1984 is the day Winston starts his ___
TRUE	17. Winston knew 2+2=4 was ____
WAR	18. Aim is to use products but not raise standard of living
POLITICAL	19. B vocabulary consists of words used for ____ purposes
CHARRINGTON	20. Runs the antique shop; really a member of the Thought Police

1984 UNIT MATCHING 1

Place the letter of the matching description from the right column on the blank in front of the number of the left column.

___ 1. EASTASIA   A. Learning, understanding, acceptance are ___ stages

___ 2. SMITH   B. B vocabulary consists of words used for ____ purposes

___ 3. PROLES   C. Responsible for economic affairs; Ministry of ___

___ 4. POWER   D. Only hope for revolution may be with them

___ 5. WAR   E. Winston bought it; it is destroyed when he is captured

___ 6. RATS   F. Enemy superstate in the middle of the novel

___ 7. POLITICAL   G. Ministry of Plenty in Newspeak

___ 8. DOWN   H. Winston knew 2+2=4 was ___

___ 9. WORDS   I. Ministry of Truth in Newspeak

___10. MINIPLENTY   J. Writing the 11th Edition of the Newspeak dictionary is____'s job

___11. TRUE   K. He is denounced by his daughter

___12. REINTEGRATION   L. Winston and Julia meet in its upstairs room; ___ shop

___13. LONDON   M. Winston's main fear and eventually his breaking point

___14. TORTURED   N. Sent to Ministry of Love for leaving the word God in a verse

___15. PLENTY   O. He doesn't believe in the Party doctrine

___16. WINSTON   P. Aim is to use products but not raise standard of living

___17. MINITRUE   Q. Ministry of Love in Newspeak

___18. MINILUV   R. A vocabulary consists of everyday ____

___19. PARSONS   S. Rewriting and distorting history was ___'s job

___20. ANTIQUE   T. Winston's diary entry: ___ with Big Brother

___21. ATOMIC   U. O'Brien _____ Winston until he believed 2+2=5

___22. PAPERWEIGHT   V. Thinking that is not allowed

___23. SYME   W. Real concept from the 1960's connected to the novel; ___ war

___24. AMPLEFORTH   X. Ultimate goal of the Party

___25. THOUGHTCRIME   Y. Setting of the novel

Copyrighted Materials

1984 UNIT MATCHING 1 KEY

Place the letter of the matching description from the right column on the blank in front of the number of the left column.

F - 1.	EASTASIA	A.	Learning, understanding, acceptance are ___ stages
S - 2.	SMITH	B.	B vocabulary consists of words used for ____ purposes
D - 3.	PROLES	C.	Responsible for economic affairs; Ministry of ___
X - 4.	POWER	D.	Only hope for revolution may be with them
P - 5.	WAR	E.	Winston bought it; it is destroyed when he is captured
M - 6.	RATS	F.	Enemy superstate in the middle of the novel
B - 7.	POLITICAL	G.	Ministry of Plenty in Newspeak
T - 8.	DOWN	H.	Winston knew 2+2=4 was ____
R - 9.	WORDS	I.	Ministry of Truth in Newspeak
G - 10.	MINIPLENTY	J.	Writing the 11th Edition of the Newspeak dictionary is ____'s job
H - 11.	TRUE	K.	He is denounced by his daughter
A - 12.	REINTEGRATION	L.	Winston and Julia meet in its upstairs room; ___ shop
Y - 13.	LONDON	M.	Winston's main fear and eventually his breaking point
U - 14.	TORTURED	N.	Sent to Ministry of Love for leaving the word God in a verse
C - 15.	PLENTY	O.	He doesn't believe in the Party doctrine
O - 16.	WINSTON	P.	Aim is to use products but not raise standard of living
I - 17.	MINITRUE	Q.	Ministry of Love in Newspeak
Q - 18.	MINILUV	R.	A vocabulary consists of everyday ____
K - 19.	PARSONS	S.	Rewriting and distorting history was ___'s job
L - 20.	ANTIQUE	T.	Winston's diary entry: ___ with Big Brother
W - 21.	ATOMIC	U.	O'Brien _____ Winston until he believed 2+2=5
E - 22.	PAPERWEIGHT	V.	Thinking that is not allowed
J - 23.	SYME	W.	Real concept from the 1960's connected to the novel; ___ war
N - 24.	AMPLEFORTH	X.	Ultimate goal of the Party
V - 25.	THOUGHTCRIME	Y.	Setting of the novel

1984 UNIT MATCHING 2

Place the letter of the matching description from the right column on the blank in front of the number of the left column.

___ 1. SLOGAN
___ 2. ORWELL
___ 3. MINILUV
___ 4. INGSOC
___ 5. PEACE
___ 6. CHILDREN
___ 7. GOLDSTEIN
___ 8. POLITICAL
___ 9. PARSONS
___ 10. TECHNICAL
___ 11. EURASIA
___ 12. TELESCREEN
___ 13. SYME
___ 14. MINIPLENTY
___ 15. JULIA
___ 16. WORDS
___ 17. AMPLEFORTH
___ 18. OLDSPEAK
___ 19. DESPAIR
___ 20. SMITH
___ 21. WAR
___ 22. ANTIQUE
___ 23. RATS
___ 24. THOUGHT
___ 25. SENSE

A. Rewriting and distorting history was ___'s job
B. Common ___ was the heresy of heresies
C. Winston and Julia meet in its upstairs room; ___ shop
D. Author of 1984
E. Ministry of Plenty in Newspeak
F. ___ Police observe and arrest people for crimes
G. Sent to Ministry of Love for leaving the word God in a verse
H. English socialism; philosophy of the Party
I. Responsible for war related events; Ministry of ___
J. Aim is to use products but not raise standard of living
K. Enemy superstate as novel opens
L. Ministry of Love in Newspeak
M. C vocabulary consists of words used in ____ fields
N. A vocabulary consists of everyday ____
O. B vocabulary consists of words used for ____ purposes
P. Hates the Party but participates enthusiastically
Q. Writing the 11th Edition of the Newspeak dictionary is ____'s job
R. Winston's main fear and eventually his breaking point
S. Two-way image and sound observation device
T. Language that is gradually being replaced
U. Enemy of the People; image used to create hatred; Emmanuel ___
V. He is denounced by his daughter
W. Mood of the novel
X. War is peace is a Party ____
Y. Taught at school to spy on parents & others

1984 UNIT MATCHING 2 KEY

Place the letter of the matching description from the right column on the blank in front of the number of the left column.

X - 1. SLOGAN	A.	Rewriting and distorting history was ___'s job
D - 2. ORWELL	B.	Common ___ was the heresy of heresies
L - 3. MINILUV	C.	Winston and Julia meet in its upstairs room; ___ shop
H - 4. INGSOC	D.	Author of 1984
I - 5. PEACE	E.	Ministry of Plenty in Newspeak
Y - 6. CHILDREN	F.	___ Police observe and arrest people for crimes
U - 7. GOLDSTEIN	G.	Sent to Ministry of Love for leaving the word God in a verse
O - 8. POLITICAL	H.	English socialism; philosophy of the Party
V - 9. PARSONS	I.	Responsible for war related events; Ministry of ___
M -10. TECHNICAL	J.	Aim is to use products but not raise standard of living
K -11. EURASIA	K.	Enemy superstate as novel opens
S -12. TELESCREEN	L.	Ministry of Love in Newspeak
Q -13. SYME	M.	C vocabulary consists of words used in ___ fields
E -14. MINIPLENTY	N.	A vocabulary consists of everyday ___
P -15. JULIA	O.	B vocabulary consists of words used for ___ purposes
N -16. WORDS	P.	Hates the Party but participates enthusiastically
G -17. AMPLEFORTH	Q.	Writing the 11th Edition of the Newspeak dictionary is___'s job
T -18. OLDSPEAK	R.	Winston's main fear and eventually his breaking point
W -19. DESPAIR	S.	Two-way image and sound observation device
A -20. SMITH	T.	Language that is gradually being replaced
J -21. WAR	U.	Enemy of the People; image used to create hatred; Emmanuel ___
C -22. ANTIQUE	V.	He is denounced by his daughter
R -23. RATS	W.	Mood of the novel
F -24. THOUGHT	X.	War is peace is a Party ___
B -25. SENSE	Y.	Taught at school to spy on parents & others

1984 UNIT MATCHING 3

Place the letter of the matching description from the right column on the blank in front of the number of the left column.

___ 1. TORTURED		A.	Winston knew 2+2=4 was ____
___ 2. CHARRINGTON		B.	English socialism; philosophy of the Party
___ 3. HATE		C.	Head of the Party; Big ___
___ 4. PAPERWEIGHT		D.	Ministry of Peace in Newspeak
___ 5. TECHNICAL		E.	Enemy superstate as novel opens
___ 6. ATOMIC		F.	Only hope for revolution may be with them
___ 7. LOVE		G.	Ministry of Plenty in Newspeak
___ 8. MINILUV		H.	C vocabulary consists of words used in ____ fields
___ 9. WAR		I.	Real concept from the 1960's connected to the novel; ___ war
___10. SCIENCE		J.	Aim is to use products but not raise standard of living
___11. MINIPAX		K.	Winston bought it; it is destroyed when he is captured
___12. WINSTON		L.	Group frenzy agains the Brotherhood; Two Minutes ____
___13. SMITH		M.	Rewriting and distorting history was ___'s job
___14. EASTASIA		N.	Maintains law and order; Ministry of ___
___15. OBRIEN		O.	Runs the antique shop; really a member of the Thought Police
___16. EURASIA		P.	O'Brien _____ Winston until he believed 2+2=5
___17. MINIPLENTY		Q.	Ministry of Love in Newspeak
___18. PARSONS		R.	Winston and Julia meet in its upstairs room; ___ shop
___19. TRUE		S.	Winston's main fear and eventually his breaking point
___20. BROTHER		T.	Re-educated Winston; wrote part of The Book
___21. INGSOC		U.	Having two contradictory thoughts at the same time
___22. PROLES		V.	Newspeak has no word for this concept
___23. RATS		W.	He is denounced by his daughter
___24. DOUBLETHINK		X.	He doesn't believe in the Party doctrine
___25. ANTIQUE		Y.	Enemy superstate in the middle of the novel

1984 UNIT MATCHING 3 KEY

Place the letter of the matching description from the right column on the blank in front of the number of the left column.

P - 1. TORTURED	A.	Winston knew 2+2=4 was ____
O - 2. CHARRINGTON	B.	English socialism; philosophy of the Party
L - 3. HATE	C.	Head of the Party; Big ____
K - 4. PAPERWEIGHT	D.	Ministry of Peace in Newspeak
H - 5. TECHNICAL	E.	Enemy superstate as novel opens
I - 6. ATOMIC	F.	Only hope for revolution may be with them
N - 7. LOVE	G.	Ministry of Plenty in Newspeak
Q - 8. MINILUV	H.	C vocabulary consists of words used in ____ fields
J - 9. WAR	I.	Real concept from the 1960's connected to the novel; ____ war
V - 10. SCIENCE	J.	Aim is to use products but not raise standard of living
D - 11. MINIPAX	K.	Winston bought it; it is destroyed when he is captured
X - 12. WINSTON	L.	Group frenzy agains the Brotherhood; Two Minutes ____
M - 13. SMITH	M.	Rewriting and distorting history was ____'s job
Y - 14. EASTASIA	N.	Maintains law and order; Ministry of ____
T - 15. OBRIEN	O.	Runs the antique shop; really a member of the Thought Police
E - 16. EURASIA	P.	O'Brien ____ Winston until he believed 2+2=5
G - 17. MINIPLENTY	Q.	Ministry of Love in Newspeak
W - 18. PARSONS	R.	Winston and Julia meet in its upstairs room; ____ shop
A - 19. TRUE	S.	Winston's main fear and eventually his breaking point
C - 20. BROTHER	T.	Re-educated Winston; wrote part of The Book
B - 21. INGSOC	U.	Having two contradictory thoughts at the same time
F - 22. PROLES	V.	Newspeak has no word for this concept
S - 23. RATS	W.	He is denounced by his daughter
U - 24. DOUBLETHINK	X.	He doesn't believe in the Party doctrine
R - 25. ANTIQUE	Y.	Enemy superstate in the middle of the novel

1984 UNIT MATCHING 4

Place the letter of the matching description from the right column on the blank in front of the number of the left column.

___ 1. PROLES	A. Newspeak has no word for this concept
___ 2. DESPAIR	B. Ministry of Plenty in Newspeak
___ 3. BROTHERHOOD	C. English socialism; philosophy of the Party
___ 4. DIARY	D. Enemy superstate as novel opens
___ 5. BOOK	E. Mood of the novel
___ 6. TECHNICAL	F. Maintains law and order; Ministry of ___
___ 7. ATOMIC	G. Responsible for news, entertainment, education, arts; Ministry of ___
___ 8. SYME	H. Winston bought it; it is destroyed when he is captured
___ 9. STRENGTH	I. Enemy superstate in the middle of the novel
___ 10. INGSOC	J. Only hope for revolution may be with them
___ 11. LOVE	K. Contains the history of the Party & the Brotherhood; The ___
___ 12. WINSTON	L. Conspirator group against the Party: The ___
___ 13. EASTASIA	M. Ignorance is ___
___ 14. DOWN	N. Speech that sounds like the quacking of a duck
___ 15. PEACE	O. He doesn't believe in the Party doctrine
___ 16. OBRIEN	P. Re-educated Winston; wrote part of The Book
___ 17. TRUTH	Q. April 4, 1984 is the day Winston starts his ___
___ 18. RATS	R. C vocabulary consists of words used in ____ fields
___ 19. MINITRUE	S. Responsible for war related events; Ministry of ___
___ 20. DUCKSPEAK	T. Winston's diary entry: ___ with Big Brother
___ 21. PLENTY	U. Writing the 11th Edition of the Newspeak dictionary is ____'s job
___ 22. SCIENCE	V. Responsible for economic affairs; Ministry of ___
___ 23. PAPERWEIGHT	W. Real concept from the 1960's connected to the novel; ___ war
___ 24. EURASIA	X. Winston's main fear and eventually his breaking point
___ 25. MINIPLENTY	Y. Ministry of Truth in Newspeak

1984 UNIT MATCHING 4 KEY

Place the letter of the matching description from the right column on the blank in front of the number of the left column.

J - 1. PROLES	A.	Newspeak has no word for this concept
E - 2. DESPAIR	B.	Ministry of Plenty in Newspeak
L - 3. BROTHERHOOD	C.	English socialism; philosophy of the Party
Q - 4. DIARY	D.	Enemy superstate as novel opens
K - 5. BOOK	E.	Mood of the novel
R - 6. TECHNICAL	F.	Maintains law and order; Ministry of ___
W - 7. ATOMIC	G.	Responsible for news, entertainment, education, arts; Ministry of ___
U - 8. SYME	H.	Winston bought it; it is destroyed when he is captured
M - 9. STRENGTH	I.	Enemy superstate in the middle of the novel
C - 10. INGSOC	J.	Only hope for revolution may be with them
F - 11. LOVE	K.	Contains the history of the Party & the Brotherhood; The ___
O - 12. WINSTON	L.	Conspirator group against the Party: The ___
I - 13. EASTASIA	M.	Ignorance is ___
T - 14. DOWN	N.	Speech that sounds like the quacking of a duck
S - 15. PEACE	O.	He doesn't believe in the Party doctrine
P - 16. OBRIEN	P.	Re-educated Winston; wrote part of The Book
G - 17. TRUTH	Q.	April 4, 1984 is the day Winston starts his ___
X - 18. RATS	R.	C vocabulary consists of words used in ___ fields
Y - 19. MINITRUE	S.	Responsible for war related events; Ministry of ___
N - 20. DUCKSPEAK	T.	Winston's diary entry: ___ with Big Brother
V - 21. PLENTY	U.	Writing the 11th Edition of the Newspeak dictionary is ___'s job
A - 22. SCIENCE	V.	Responsible for economic affairs; Ministry of ___
H - 23. PAPERWEIGHT	W.	Real concept from the 1960's connected to the novel; ___ war
D - 24. EURASIA	X.	Winston's main fear and eventually his breaking point
B - 25. MINIPLENTY	Y.	Ministry of Truth in Newspeak

Copyrighted Materials

1984 UNIT MAGIC SQUARES 1

Match the definition with the vocabulary word. Put your answers in the magic squares below. When your answers are correct, all columns and rows will add to the same number.

A. ORWELL
B. WATCHING
C. JULIA
D. LOVE
E. SENSE
F. MINIPLENTY

G. DIVORCE
H. OBRIEN
I. SLOGAN
J. DESPAIR
K. INGSOC
L. AMPLEFORTH

M. SMITH
N. BOOK
O. PLENTY
P. LONDON

1. Big Brother is _____ you
2. Not allowed by the Party
3. English socialism; philosophy of the Party
4. Contains the history of the Party & the Brotherhood; The ___
5. Rewriting and distorting history was ___'s job
6. Sent to Ministry of Love for leaving the word God in a verse
7. Re-educated Winston; wrote part of The Book
8. Author of 1984
9. Setting of the novel
10. War is peace is a Party ____
11. Common ___ was the heresy of heresies
12. Maintains law and order; Ministry of ___
13. Hates the Party but participates enthusiastically
14. Ministry of Plenty in Newspeak
15. Mood of the novel
16. Responsible for economic affairs; Ministry of ___

A=	B=	C=	D=
E=	F=	G=	H=
I=	J=	K=	L=
M=	N=	O=	P=

1984 UNIT MATCHING SQUARES 1 KEY

Match the definition with the vocabulary word. Put your answers in the magic squares below. When your answers are correct, all columns and rows will add to the same number.

A. ORWELL
B. WATCHING
C. JULIA
D. LOVE
E. SENSE
F. MINIPLENTY
G. DIVORCE
H. OBRIEN
I. SLOGAN
J. DESPAIR
K. INGSOC
L. AMPLEFORTH
M. SMITH
N. BOOK
O. PLENTY
P. LONDON

1. Big Brother is _____ you
2. Not allowed by the Party
3. English socialism; philosophy of the Party
4. Contains the history of the Party & the Brotherhood; The ___
5. Rewriting and distorting history was ___'s job
6. Sent to Ministry of Love for leaving the word God in a verse
7. Re-educated Winston; wrote part of The Book
8. Author of 1984
9. Setting of the novel
10. War is peace is a Party ____
11. Common ___ was the heresy of heresies
12. Maintains law and order; Ministry of ___
13. Hates the Party but participates enthusiastically
14. Ministry of Plenty in Newspeak
15. Mood of the novel
16. Responsible for economic affairs; Ministry of ___

A=8	B=1	C=13	D=12
E=11	F=14	G=2	H=7
I=10	J=15	K=3	L=6
M=5	N=4	O=16	P=9

1984 UNIT MATCHING SQUARES 2

Match the definition with the vocabulary word. Put your answers in the magic squares below. When your answers are correct, all columns and rows will add to the same number.

A. TRUTH
B. ORWELL
C. TRUE
D. TELESCREEN
E. TORTURED
F. SCIENCE
G. MINILUV
H. DIVORCE
I. NEWSPEAK
J. STRENGTH
K. THOUGHTCRIME
L. DOWN
M. PLENTY
N. HATE
O. DOUBLETHINK
P. OLDSPEAK

1. Newspeak has no word for this concept
2. Language that narrows the range of thought
3. Having two contradictory thoughts at the same time
4. Two-way image and sound observation device
5. Responsible for economic affairs; Ministry of ___
6. Author of 1984
7. Not allowed by the Party
8. Thinking that is not allowed
9. Winston knew 2+2=4 was ___
10. Language that is gradually being replaced
11. Ignorance is ___
12. O'Brien _____ Winston until he believed 2+2=5
13. Winston's diary entry: ___ with Big Brother
14. Ministry of Love in Newspeak
15. Responsible for news, entertainment, education, arts; Ministry of ___
16. Group frenzy agains the Brotherhood; Two Minutes ___

A=	B=	C=	D=
E=	F=	G=	H=
I=	J=	K=	L=
M=	N=	O=	P=

1984 UNIT MATCHING SQUARES 2 KEY

Match the definition with the vocabulary word. Put your answers in the magic squares below. When your answers are correct, all columns and rows will add to the same number.

A. TRUTH
B. ORWELL
C. TRUE
D. TELESCREEN
E. TORTURED
F. SCIENCE
G. MINILUV
H. DIVORCE
I. NEWSPEAK
J. STRENGTH
K. THOUGHTCRIME
L. DOWN
M. PLENTY
N. HATE
O. DOUBLETHINK
P. OLDSPEAK

1. Newspeak has no word for this concept
2. Language that narrows the range of thought
3. Having two contradictory thoughts at the same time
4. Two-way image and sound observation device
5. Responsible for economic affairs; Ministry of ___
6. Author of 1984
7. Not allowed by the Party
8. Thinking that is not allowed
9. Winston knew 2+2=4 was ___
10. Language that is gradually being replaced
11. Ignorance is ___
12. O'Brien ___ Winston until he believed 2+2=5
13. Winston's diary entry: ___ with Big Brother
14. Ministry of Love in Newspeak
15. Responsible for news, entertainment, education, arts; Ministry of ___
16. Group frenzy agains the Brotherhood; Two Minutes ___

A=15	B=6	C=9	D=4
E=12	F=1	G=14	H=7
I=2	J=11	K=8	L=13
M=5	N=16	O=3	P=10

25
Copyrighted Materials

1984 UNIT MATCHING SQUARES 3

Match the definition with the vocabulary word. Put your answers in the magic squares below. When your answers are correct, all columns and rows will add to the same number.

A. DUCKSPEAK	G. TELESCREEN	M. DIARY
B. NEWSPEAK	H. THOUGHT	N. SCIENCE
C. BROTHER	I. LONDON	O. WAR
D. WATCHING	J. INGSOC	P. PEACE
E. DOUBLETHINK	K. PLENTY
F. SENSE	L. TECHNICAL

1. Speech that sounds like the quacking of a duck
2. Newspeak has no word for this concept
3. English socialism; philosophy of the Party
4. Having two contradictory thoughts at the same time
5. Two-way image and sound observation device
6. C vocabulary consists of words used in ____ fields
7. Responsible for war related events; Ministry of ___
8. Head of the Party; Big ___
9. Aim is to use products but not raise standard of living
10. Big Brother is _____ you
11. ___ Police observe and arrest people for crimes
12. Responsible for economic affairs; Ministry of ___
13. Setting of the novel
14. Common ___ was the heresy of heresies
15. Language that narrows the range of thought
16. April 4, 1984 is the day Winston starts his ___

A=	B=	C=	D=
E=	F=	G=	H=
I=	J=	K=	L=
M=	N=	O=	P=

1984 UNIT MATCHING SQUARES 3 KEY

Match the definition with the vocabulary word. Put your answers in the magic squares below. When your answers are correct, all columns and rows will add to the same number.

A. DUCKSPEAK
B. NEWSPEAK
C. BROTHER
D. WATCHING
E. DOUBLETHINK
F. SENSE
G. TELESCREEN
H. THOUGHT
I. LONDON
J. INGSOC
K. PLENTY
L. TECHNICAL
M. DIARY
N. SCIENCE
O. WAR
P. PEACE

1. Speech that sounds like the quacking of a duck
2. Newspeak has no word for this concept
3. English socialism; philosophy of the Party
4. Having two contradictory thoughts at the same time
5. Two-way image and sound observation device
6. C vocabulary consists of words used in ____ fields
7. Responsible for war related events; Ministry of ___
8. Head of the Party; Big ___
9. Aim is to use products but not raise standard of living
10. Big Brother is _____ you
11. ___ Police observe and arrest people for crimes
12. Responsible for economic affairs; Ministry of ___
13. Setting of the novel
14. Common ___ was the heresy of heresies
15. Language that narrows the range of thought
16. April 4, 1984 is the day Winston starts his ___

A=1	B=15	C=8	D=10
E=4	F=14	G=5	H=11
I=13	J=3	K=12	L=6
M=16	N=2	O=9	P=7

1984 UNIT MATCHING SQUARES 4

Match the definition with the vocabulary word. Put your answers in the magic squares below. When your answers are correct, all columns and rows will add to the same number.

A. POWER
B. SMITH
C. POLITICAL
D. AMPLEFORTH
E. DUCKSPEAK
F. FACECRIME
G. MINILUV
H. SCIENCE
I. WINSTON
J. MINITRUE
K. PAPERWEIGHT
L. CHARRINGTON
M. REINTEGRATION
N. EASTASIA
O. DIARY
P. OBRIEN

1. B vocabulary consists of words used for ____ purposes
2. Ministry of Truth in Newspeak
3. Having the wrong look on one's features
4. April 4, 1984 is the day Winston starts his ___
5. Re-educated Winston; wrote part of The Book
6. Speech that sounds like the quacking of a duck
7. He doesn't believe in the Party doctrine
8. Sent to Ministry of Love for leaving the word God in a verse
9. Learning, understanding, acceptance are ___ stages
10. Newspeak has no word for this concept
11. Runs the antique shop; really a member of the Thought Police
12. Ultimate goal of the Party
13. Rewriting and distorting history was ___'s job
14. Winston bought it; it is destroyed when he is captured
15. Ministry of Love in Newspeak
16. Enemy superstate in the middle of the novel

A=	B=	C=	D=
E=	F=	G=	H=
I=	J=	K=	L=
M=	N=	O=	P=

1984 UNIT MATCHING SQUARES 4 KEY

Match the definition with the vocabulary word. Put your answers in the magic squares below. When your answers are correct, all columns and rows will add to the same number.

A. POWER
B. SMITH
C. POLITICAL
D. AMPLEFORTH
E. DUCKSPEAK
F. FACECRIME
G. MINILUV
H. SCIENCE
I. WINSTON
J. MINITRUE
K. PAPERWEIGHT
L. CHARRINGTON
M. REINTEGRATION
N. EASTASIA
O. DIARY
P. OBRIEN

1. B vocabulary consists of words used for ____ purposes
2. Ministry of Truth in Newspeak
3. Having the wrong look on one's features
4. April 4, 1984 is the day Winston starts his ___
5. Re-educated Winston; wrote part of The Book
6. Speech that sounds like the quacking of a duck
7. He doesn't believe in the Party doctrine
8. Sent to Ministry of Love for leaving the word God in a verse
9. Learning, understanding, acceptance are ___ stages
10. Newspeak has no word for this concept
11. Runs the antique shop; really a member of the Thought Police
12. Ultimate goal of the Party
13. Rewriting and distorting history was ___'s job
14. Winston bought it; it is destroyed when he is captured
15. Ministry of Love in Newspeak
16. Enemy superstate in the middle of the novel

A=12	B=13	C=1	D=8
E=6	F=3	G=15	H=10
I=7	J=2	K=14	L=11
M=9	N=16	O=4	P=5

1984 UNIT WORD SEARCH 1

Words are placed backwards, forward, diagonally, up and down. Clues listed below can help you find the words. Circle the hidden vocabulary words in the maze.

```
T H O U G H T S D R O W S L A V E R Y G
E S N E S Z T O L Q D F A I M T W E T T
L C N L D A P C B O Z Q S R I O I H N C
E I E C R E A E P G G A X S N R N T E G
S E R R V G R A O C R A N H I T S O L T
C N D O P B S N W U M X N X L U T R P Y
R C L I Z A O I E W I D A C U R O B I Z
E E I V V W N A R M N P T I V E N Y N F
E N H H H O S T M C I H N M F D V T I V
N E C T B J R K I N T F A O D E L N M S
G I U B O O K C I Q R E R T C L O E E S
Y R A I D S Y M E J U L I A E D Q L L R
T B D C O S G N I R E E E W N R O P P V
V O C H W S M I T H J P R O R R H C C G
S T R E N G T H S J W O L N P P K C S G
```

A vocabulary consists of everyday ____ (5)
Aim is to use products but not raise standard of living (3)
April 4, 1984 is the day Winston starts his ___ (5)
Author of 1984 (6)
Common ___ was the heresy of heresies (5)
Contains the history of the Party & the Brotherhood; The ___ (4)
Enemy superstate as novel opens (7)
English socialism; philosophy of the Party (6)
Freedom is ___ (7)
Group frenzy agains the Brotherhood; Two Minutes ____ (4)
Hates the Party but participates enthusiastically (5)
He doesn't believe in the Party doctrine (7)
He is denounced by his daughter (7)
Head of the Party; Big ___ (7)
Ignorance is ___ (8)
Maintains law and order; Ministry of ___ (4)
Ministry of Love in Newspeak (7)
Ministry of Peace in Newspeak (7)
Ministry of Plenty in Newspeak (10)
Ministry of Truth in Newspeak (8)
Newspeak has no word for this concept (7)
Not allowed by the Party (7)
O'Brien _____ Winston until he believed 2+2=5 (8)
Only hope for revolution may be with them (6)

Re-educated Winston; wrote part of The Book (6)
Real concept from the 1960's connected to the novel; ___ war (6)
Responsible for economic affairs; Ministry of ___ (6)
Responsible for news, entertainment, education, arts; Ministry of ___ (5)
Responsible for war related events; Ministry of ___ (5)
Rewriting and distorting history was ___'s job (5)
Setting of the novel (6)
Superstate ruled by the Party (7)
Taught at school to spy on parents & others (8)
Two-way image and sound observation device (10)
Ultimate goal of the Party (5)
War is peace is a Party ____ (6)
Winston and Julia meet in its upstairs room; ___ shop (7)
Winston knew 2+2=4 was ____ (4)
Winston's diary entry: ___ with Big Brother (4)
Winston's main fear and eventually his breaking point (4)
Writing the 11th Edition of the Newspeak dictionary is____'s job (4)
___ Police observe and arrest people for crimes (7)

1984 UNIT WORD SEARCH 1 KEY

Words are placed backwards, forward, diagonally, up and down. Clues listed below can help you find the words. Circle the hidden vocabulary words in the maze.

A vocabulary consists of everyday ____ (5)
Aim is to use products but not raise standard of living (3)
April 4, 1984 is the day Winston starts his ____ (5)
Author of 1984 (6)
Common ____ was the heresy of heresies (5)
Contains the history of the Party & the Brotherhood; The ____ (4)
Enemy superstate as novel opens (7)
English socialism; philosophy of the Party (6)
Freedom is ____ (7)
Group frenzy agains the Brotherhood; Two Minutes ____ (4)
Hates the Party but participates enthusiastically (5)
He doesn't believe in the Party doctrine (7)
He is denounced by his daughter (7)
Head of the Party; Big ____ (7)
Ignorance is ____ (8)
Maintains law and order; Ministry of ____ (4)
Ministry of Love in Newspeak (7)
Ministry of Peace in Newspeak (7)
Ministry of Plenty in Newspeak (10)
Ministry of Truth in Newspeak (8)
Newspeak has no word for this concept (7)
Not allowed by the Party (7)
O'Brien ____ Winston until he believed 2+2=5 (8)
Only hope for revolution may be with them (6)

Re-educated Winston; wrote part of The Book (6)
Real concept from the 1960's connected to the novel; ____ war (6)
Responsible for economic affairs; Ministry of ____ (6)
Responsible for news, entertainment, education, arts; Ministry of ____ (5)
Responsible for war related events; Ministry of ____ (5)
Rewriting and distorting history was ____'s job (5)
Setting of the novel (6)
Superstate ruled by the Party (7)
Taught at school to spy on parents & others (8)
Two-way image and sound observation device (10)
Ultimate goal of the Party (5)
War is peace is a Party ____ (6)
Winston and Julia meet in its upstairs room; ____ shop (7)
Winston knew 2+2=4 was ____ (4)
Winston's diary entry: ____ with Big Brother (4)
Winston's main fear and eventually his breaking point (4)
Writing the 11th Edition of the Newspeak dictionary is ____'s job (4)
____ Police observe and arrest people for crimes (7)

1984 UNIT WORD SEARCH 2

Words are placed backwards, forward, diagonally, up and down. Clues listed below can help you find the words. Circle the hidden vocabulary words in the maze.

```
T P S M I T H O N S N E W S P E A K W V
R N O D N O L B V N E R D L I H C N R C
U K B S G D A R W K H P E A C E F I I R
E W C R S T V I A A N W X D T M E A M
J S E L O R P E A S T A S I A W X T P C
W Y X M C T P N R Y E C A X N Z S S S N
N Z I V H S H K O G W R H R H S B D E V
B C R E K T O E B L Y O N I Z R T L D D
F A V C Z O R U R R D W R S N R H O R G
W O U D B R W Q E H O S R D U G O G N N
L D L Z B T E I W D O T P T S S U J J L
W Q I K N U L T O S B O H E P H G U F K
S E N S E R L N P Y F Z D E A J H L H F
E M I R C E C A F M G X L N R K T I B F
N K M X D D S C I E N C E S L O G A N J
```

A vocabulary consists of everyday ____ (5)
Aim is to use products but not raise standard of living (3)
April 4, 1984 is the day Winston starts his ___ (5)
Author of 1984 (6)
Big Brother is _____ you (8)
Common ___ was the heresy of heresies (5)
Conspirator group against the Party: The ___ (11)
Contains the history of the Party & the Brotherhood; The ___ (4)
Enemy of the People; image used to create hatred; Emmanuel ___ (9)
Enemy superstate in the middle of the novel (8)
English socialism; philosophy of the Party (6)
Group frenzy agains the Brotherhood; Two Minutes ____ (4)
Hates the Party but participates enthusiastically (5)
Having the wrong look on one's features (9)
He doesn't believe in the Party doctrine (7)
Head of the Party; Big ___ (7)
Language that is gradually being replaced (8)
Language that narrows the range of thought (8)
Maintains law and order; Ministry of ___ (4)
Ministry of Love in Newspeak (7)
Mood of the novel (7)
Newspeak has no word for this concept (7)
O'Brien _____ Winston until he believed 2+2=5 (8)

Only hope for revolution may be with them (6)
Re-educated Winston; wrote part of The Book (6)
Real concept from the 1960's connected to the novel; ___ war (6)
Responsible for economic affairs; Ministry of ___ (6)
Responsible for news, entertainment, education, arts; Ministry of ___ (5)
Responsible for war related events; Ministry of ___ (5)
Rewriting and distorting history was ___'s job (5)
Setting of the novel (6)
Speech that sounds like the quacking of a duck (9)
Taught at school to spy on parents & others (8)
Ultimate goal of the Party (5)
War is peace is a Party ____ (6)
Winston and Julia meet in its upstairs room; ___ shop (7)
Winston knew 2+2=4 was ____ (4)
Winston's diary entry: ___ with Big Brother (4)
Winston's main fear and eventually his breaking point (4)
Writing the 11th Edition of the Newspeak dictionary is____'s job (4)
___ Police observe and arrest people for crimes (7)

1984 UNIT WORD SEARCH 2 KEY

Words are placed backwards, forward, diagonally, up and down. Clues listed below can help you find the words. Circle the hidden vocabulary words in the maze.

```
T     S M I T H O     N E W S P E A K
R N O D N O L B   N E R D L I H C N R
U   B   G   A R W K H P E A C E   I   R
E       R S T   I A A N   W D     E   A
  S E L O R P E A S T A S I A     T   P
        M C T P N   Y E C A   N   S S S
        I     S H K O   W R H     S   D E
      C R E K T O E B L Y O N I     T L D
      A V C   O R U R R D W R   N R H O
W O U     B R W Q E H O S   D U G O G N
L D L       T E I W D O T P T S   U J
    I       U L T O S   O H E     G U
  S E N S E R L N P Y     D E A   H L
E M I   R C E C A F M         R K T I
    M         D S C I E N C E S L O G A N
```

A vocabulary consists of everyday ____ (5)
Aim is to use products but not raise standard of living (3)
April 4, 1984 is the day Winston starts his ___ (5)
Author of 1984 (6)
Big Brother is _____ you (8)
Common ___ was the heresy of heresies (5)
Conspirator group against the Party: The ___ (11)
Contains the history of the Party & the Brotherhood; The ___ (4)
Enemy of the People; image used to create hatred; Emmanuel ___ (9)
Enemy superstate in the middle of the novel (8)
English socialism; philosophy of the Party (6)
Group frenzy agains the Brotherhood; Two Minutes ___ (4)
Hates the Party but participates enthusiastically (5)
Having the wrong look on one's features (9)
He doesn't believe in the Party doctrine (7)
Head of the Party; Big ___ (7)
Language that is gradually being replaced (8)
Language that narrows the range of thought (8)
Maintains law and order; Ministry of ___ (4)
Ministry of Love in Newspeak (7)
Mood of the novel (7)
Newspeak has no word for this concept (7)
O'Brien _____ Winston until he believed 2+2=5 (8)

Only hope for revolution may be with them (6)
Re-educated Winston; wrote part of The Book (6)
Real concept from the 1960's connected to the novel; ___ war (6)
Responsible for economic affairs; Ministry of ___ (6)
Responsible for news, entertainment, education, arts; Ministry of ___ (5)
Responsible for war related events; Ministry of ___ (5)
Rewriting and distorting history was ___'s job (5)
Setting of the novel (6)
Speech that sounds like the quacking of a duck (9)
Taught at school to spy on parents & others (8)
Ultimate goal of the Party (5)
War is peace is a Party ____ (6)
Winston and Julia meet in its upstairs room; ___ shop (7)
Winston knew 2+2=4 was ____ (4)
Winston's diary entry: ___ with Big Brother (4)
Winston's main fear and eventually his breaking point (4)
Writing the 11th Edition of the Newspeak dictionary is____'s job (4)
___ Police observe and arrest people for crimes (7)

1984 UNIT WORD SEARCH 3

Words are placed backwards, forward, diagonally, up and down. Words listed below are included in the maze. Circle the hidden vocabulary words in the maze.

I	N	G	S	O	C	Y	D	S	S	T	A	T	O	M	I	C	D	F	S
D	E	S	P	A	I	R	B	E	P	H	P	O	S	Q	S	S	I	E	C
V	O	C	E	A	N	I	A	L	B	O	F	R	V	D	F	L	V	M	R
J	U	L	I	A	A	R	L	O	E	U	W	W	R	U	H	A	O	I	N
Y	C	K	P	H	G	D	Y	R	T	G	G	E	W	C	D	V	R	R	Z
P	M	N	T	O	O	N	B	P	A	H	H	L	R	K	W	E	C	C	C
N	M	I	N	I	L	U	V	O	H	T	E	L	E	S	C	R	E	E	N
S	M	H	N	E	S	I	F	W	O	R	S	C	D	P	Y	Y	S	C	K
S	A	T	E	I	A	V	T	R	R	K	H	R	G	E	W	M	N	A	D
L	N	E	D	U	T	S	B	I	N	W	O	D	C	A	A	B	E	F	Y
O	T	L	L	I	R	R	T	H	C	W	H	H	X	K	R	P	S	T	R
N	I	B	O	D	A	A	U	A	X	A	E	M	X	R	S	W	H	R	T
D	Q	U	V	C	F	R	S	E	S	U	L	R	V	D	G	W	W	U	L
O	U	O	E	L	Q	C	Y	I	R	I	T	G	L	P	L	E	N	T	Y
N	E	D	P	E	A	C	E	T	A	R	A	O	B	R	I	E	N	H	M

ANTIQUE	DUCKSPEAK	MINILUV	POWER	THOUGHT
ATOMIC	EASTASIA	MINITRUE	PROLES	TRUE
BOOK	EURASIA	OBRIEN	RATS	TRUTH
BROTHER	FACECRIME	OCEANIA	SENSE	WAR
DESPAIR	HATE	OLDSPEAK	SLAVERY	WORDS
DIARY	INGSOC	ORWELL	SLOGAN	
DIVORCE	JULIA	PEACE	SMITH	
DOUBLETHINK	LONDON	PLENTY	SYME	
DOWN	LOVE	POLITICAL	TELESCREEN	

1984 UNIT WORD SEARCH 3 KEY

Words are placed backwards, forward, diagonally, up and down. Words listed below are included in the maze. Circle the hidden vocabulary words in the maze.

ANTIQUE	DUCKSPEAK	MINILUV	POWER	THOUGHT
ATOMIC	EASTASIA	MINITRUE	PROLES	TRUE
BOOK	EURASIA	OBRIEN	RATS	TRUTH
BROTHER	FACECRIME	OCEANIA	SENSE	WAR
DESPAIR	HATE	OLDSPEAK	SLAVERY	WORDS
DIARY	INGSOC	ORWELL	SLOGAN	
DIVORCE	JULIA	PEACE	SMITH	
DOUBLETHINK	LONDON	PLENTY	SYME	
DOWN	LOVE	POLITICAL	TELESCREEN	

1984 UNIT WORD SEARCH 4

Words are placed backwards, forward, diagonally, up and down. Words listed below are included in the maze. Circle the hidden vocabulary words in the maze.

```
W I N S T O N P S F T E N W O D E M Y S
M I N I P A X L R G R B A R Y E C M L B
N V Y P B E A D Z O O Y O S M S T O T D
E P W R N V U N O N L L O T P G R R W
I A B Y E T O R T U R E D P K A I L U J
R P M R R I A Z A N B U S S N I S N T E
B E Y P D W N T Y S C L P M T R E I H Y
O R W E L L A G O K I X E N C E S T A R
C W O C I E J R S M K A A T R S I B T F
P E R R H Z F P L O I K K C H C S N E J
L I D O C B E O V O C C S H C I E X K W
E G S V T A J W R L V E S T R E N G T H
N H L I K K H E G T L E Z I R N S K N S
T T M D D I A R Y E H C L M R C E J N Q
Y P E A C E N T T K A E P S W E N N X P
```

AMPLEFORTH	DUCKSPEAK	NEWSPEAK	RATS	TORTURED
ATOMIC	EASTASIA	OBRIEN	SCIENCE	TRUE
BOOK	EURASIA	OLDSPEAK	SENSE	TRUTH
CHILDREN	GOLDSTEIN	ORWELL	SLAVERY	WAR
DESPAIR	HATE	PAPERWEIGHT	SLOGAN	WINSTON
DIARY	INGSOC	PEACE	SMITH	WORDS
DIVORCE	JULIA	PLENTY	STRENGTH	
DOUBLETHINK	LOVE	POWER	SYME	
DOWN	MINIPAX	PROLES	TELESCREEN	

36
Copyrighted Materials

1984 UNIT WORD SEARCH 4 KEY

Words are placed backwards, forward, diagonally, up and down. Words listed below are included in the maze. Circle the hidden vocabulary words in the maze.

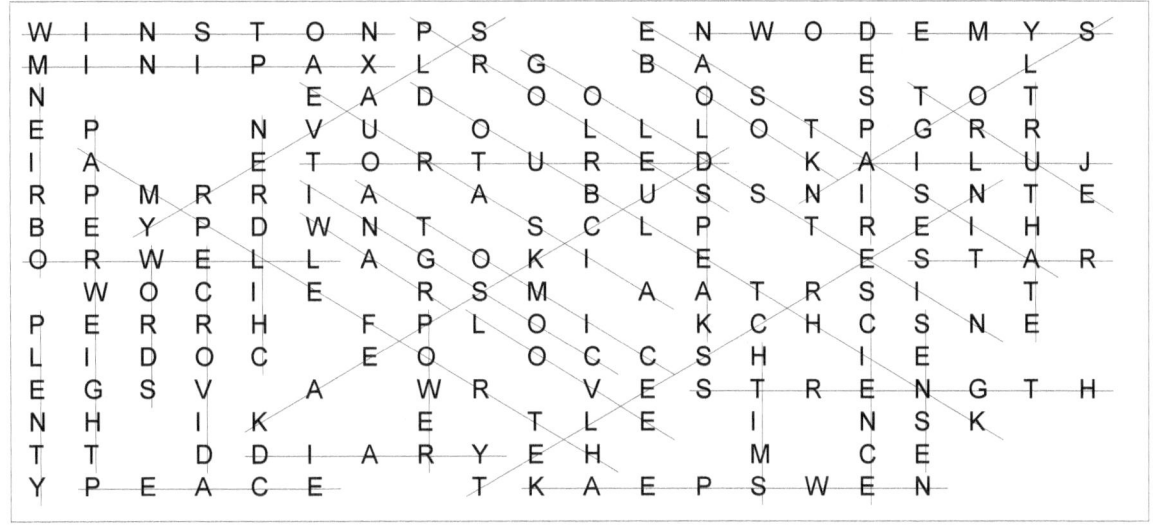

AMPLEFORTH	DUCKSPEAK	NEWSPEAK	RATS	TORTURED
ATOMIC	EASTASIA	OBRIEN	SCIENCE	TRUE
BOOK	EURASIA	OLDSPEAK	SENSE	TRUTH
CHILDREN	GOLDSTEIN	ORWELL	SLAVERY	WAR
DESPAIR	HATE	PAPERWEIGHT	SLOGAN	WINSTON
DIARY	INGSOC	PEACE	SMITH	WORDS
DIVORCE	JULIA	PLENTY	STRENGTH	
DOUBLETHINK	LOVE	POWER	SYME	
DOWN	MINIPAX	PROLES	TELESCREEN	

1984 UNIT CROSSWORD 1

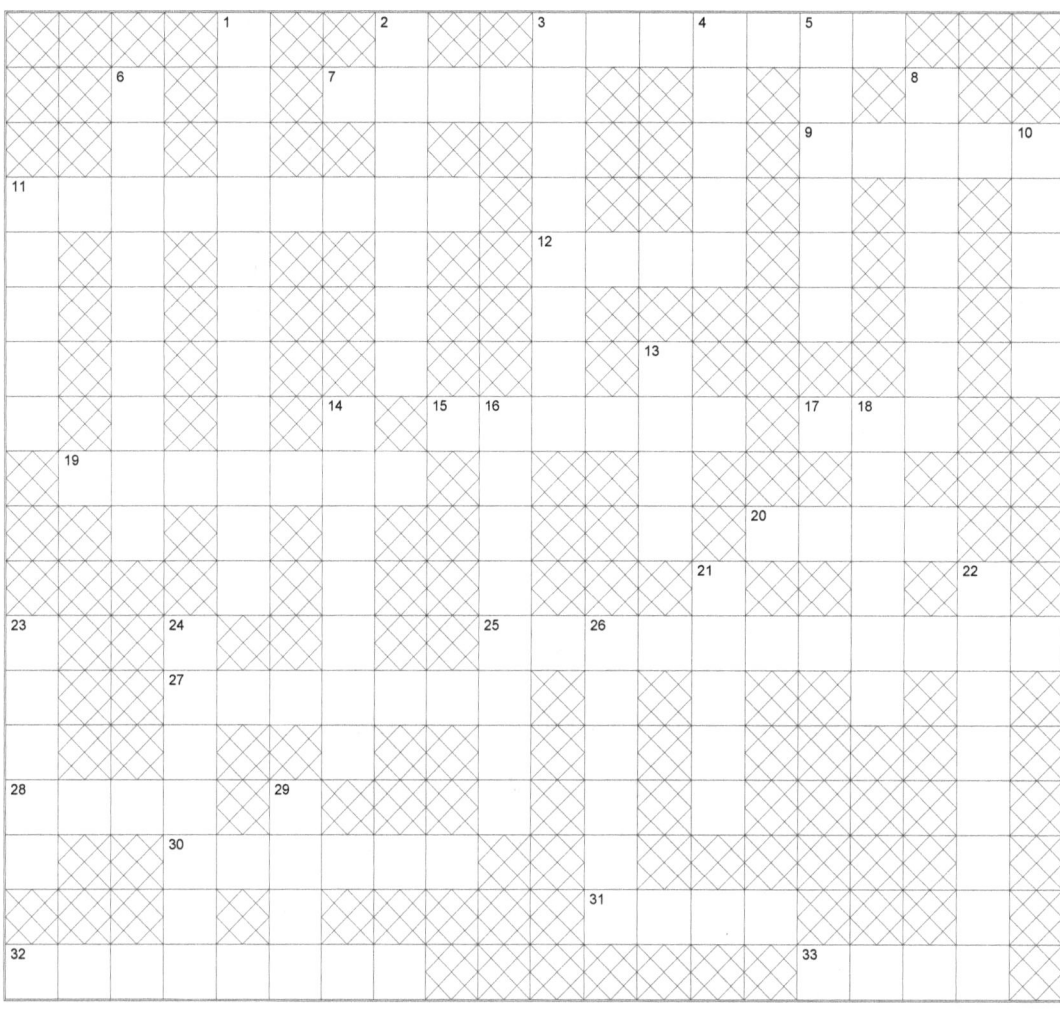

Across
3. He doesn't believe in the Party doctrine
7. Hates the Party but participates enthusiastically
9. A vocabulary consists of everyday ____
11. B vocabulary consists of words used for ____ purposes
12. Group frenzy agains the Brotherhood; Two Minutes ____
15. English socialism; philosophy of the Party
17. Aim is to use products but not raise standard of living
19. Not allowed by the Party
20. Contains the history of the Party & the Brotherhood; The ____
25. Winston bought it; it is destroyed when he is captured
27. Winston and Julia meet in its upstairs room; ____ shop
28. Winston's main fear and eventually his breaking point
30. Re-educated Winston; wrote part of The Book
31. Writing the 11th Edition of the Newspeak dictionary is ____'s job
32. Language that is gradually being replaced
33. Winston's diary entry: ____ with Big Brother

Down
1. Conspirator group against the Party: The ____
2. Enemy superstate as novel opens
3. Big Brother is ____ you
4. Common ____ was the heresy of heresies
5. Author of 1984
6. Enemy of the People; image used to create hatred; Emmanuel ____
8. Head of the Party; Big ____
10. Rewriting and distorting history was ____'s job
11. Responsible for war related events; Ministry of ____
13. Maintains law and order; Ministry of ____
14. Superstate ruled by the Party
16. Language that narrows the range of thought
18. Real concept from the 1960's connected to the novel; ____ war
21. Responsible for news, entertainment, education, arts; Ministry of ____
22. Taught at school to spy on parents & others
23. April 4, 1984 is the day Winston starts his ____
24. He is denounced by his daughter
26. Only hope for revolution may be with them
29. Winston knew 2+2=4 was ____

1984 UNIT CROSSWORD 1 KEY

Across
3. He doesn't believe in the Party doctrine
7. Hates the Party but participates enthusiastically
9. A vocabulary consists of everyday ____
11. B vocabulary consists of words used for ____ purposes
12. Group frenzy agains the Brotherhood; Two Minutes ____
15. English socialism; philosophy of the Party
17. Aim is to use products but not raise standard of living
19. Not allowed by the Party
20. Contains the history of the Party & the Brotherhood; The ____
25. Winston bought it; it is destroyed when he is captured
27. Winston and Julia meet in its upstairs room; ____ shop
28. Winston's main fear and eventually his breaking point
30. Re-educated Winston; wrote part of The Book
31. Writing the 11th Edition of the Newspeak dictionary is____'s job
32. Language that is gradually being replaced
33. Winston's diary entry: ____ with Big Brother

Down
1. Conspirator group against the Party: The ____
2. Enemy superstate as novel opens
3. Big Brother is ____ you
4. Common ____ was the heresy of heresies
5. Author of 1984
6. Enemy of the People; image used to create hatred; Emmanuel ____
8. Head of the Party; Big ____
10. Rewriting and distorting history was ____'s job
11. Responsible for war related events; Ministry of ____
13. Maintains law and order; Ministry of ____
14. Superstate ruled by the Party
16. Language that narrows the range of thought
18. Real concept from the 1960's connected to the novel; ____ war
21. Responsible for news, entertainment, education, arts; Ministry of ____
22. Taught at school to spy on parents & others
23. April 4, 1984 is the day Winston starts his ____
24. He is denounced by his daughter
26. Only hope for revolution may be with them
29. Winston knew 2+2=4 was ____

1984 UNIT CROSSWORD 2

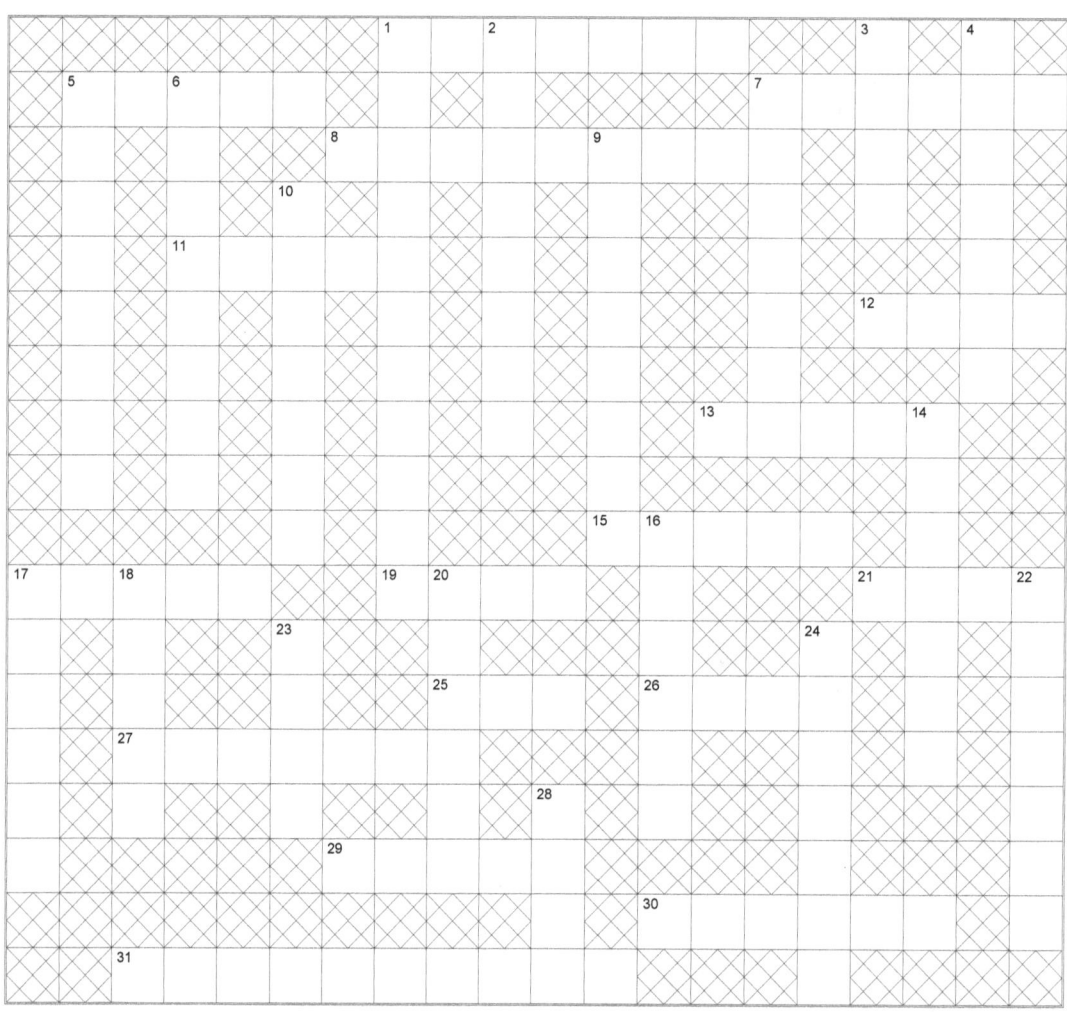

Across
1. Head of the Party; Big ___
5. Common ___ was the heresy of heresies
7. Real concept from the 1960's connected to the novel; ___ war
8. Enemy of the People; image used to create hatred; Emmanuel ___
11. Rewriting and distorting history was ___'s job
12. Winston knew 2+2=4 was ___
13. Responsible for war related events; Ministry of ___
15. April 4, 1984 is the day Winston starts his ___
17. Ultimate goal of the Party
19. Winston's diary entry: ___ with Big Brother
21. Winston's main fear and eventually his breaking point
25. Aim is to use products but not raise standard of living
26. Writing the 11th Edition of the Newspeak dictionary is____'s job
27. Not allowed by the Party
29. Hates the Party but participates enthusiastically
30. Re-educated Winston; wrote part of The Book
31. Two-way image and sound observation device

Down
1. Conspirator group against the Party: The ___
2. Language that is gradually being replaced
3. Maintains law and order; Ministry of ___
4. Ministry of Love in Newspeak
5. Ignorance is ___
6. Language that narrows the range of thought
7. Winston and Julia meet in its upstairs room; ___ shop
9. O'Brien _____ Winston until he believed 2+2=5
10. He doesn't believe in the Party doctrine
14. Enemy superstate as novel opens
16. English socialism; philosophy of the Party
17. Only hope for revolution may be with them
18. A vocabulary consists of everyday ____
20. Author of 1984
22. Freedom is ___
23. Contains the history of the Party & the Brotherhood; The ___
24. Mood of the novel
28. Group frenzy agains the Brotherhood; Two Minutes ____

1984 UNIT CROSSWORD 2 KEY

					¹B	²R	O	T	H	E	R		³L		⁴M	
	⁵S	E	⁶N	S	E		L					⁷A	T	O	M	I	C
	T		E			⁸G	O	L	D	⁹S	T	E	I	N		N
	R		W		¹⁰W		T		S		O		T		E		I
	E		¹¹S	M	I	T	H		P		R		I			¹²T	R	U	E
	N		P		N		E		E		T		Q		
	G		E		S		R		A		U		¹³U		¹⁴E
	T		A		T		H		K		R		P	E	A	C	E
	H		K		O		O				E				U
					N		O			¹⁵D	¹⁶I	A	R	Y		R
¹⁷P	¹⁸O	W	E	R		¹⁹D	²⁰O	W	N		N			²¹R	A	T	²²S
R		O			²³B		R				G		²⁴D		S		L
O		R			O		²⁵W	A	R		²⁶S	Y	M	E		I	A
L		²⁷D	I	V	O	R	C	E			O		S		A		V
E		S			K		L		²⁸H		C		P				E
S					²⁹J	U	L	I	A				A				R
									T		³⁰O	B	R	I	E	N	Y
		³¹T	E	L	E	S	C	R	E	E	N		R		

Across

1. Head of the Party; Big ___
5. Common ___ was the heresy of heresies
7. Real concept from the 1960's connected to the novel; ___ war
8. Enemy of the People; image used to create hatred; Emmanuel ___
11. Rewriting and distorting history was ___'s job
12. Winston knew 2+2=4 was ___
13. Responsible for war related events; Ministry of ___
15. April 4, 1984 is the day Winston starts his ___
17. Ultimate goal of the Party
19. Winston's diary entry: ___ with Big Brother
21. Winston's main fear and eventually his breaking point
25. Aim is to use products but not raise standard of living
26. Writing the 11th Edition of the Newspeak dictionary is___'s job
27. Not allowed by the Party
29. Hates the Party but participates enthusiastically
30. Re-educated Winston; wrote part of The Book
31. Two-way image and sound observation device

Down

1. Conspirator group against the Party: The ___
2. Language that is gradually being replaced
3. Maintains law and order; Ministry of ___
4. Ministry of Love in Newspeak
5. Ignorance is ___
6. Language that narrows the range of thought
7. Winston and Julia meet in its upstairs room; ___ shop
9. O'Brien _____ Winston until he believed 2+2=5
10. He doesn't believe in the Party doctrine
14. Enemy superstate as novel opens
16. English socialism; philosophy of the Party
17. Only hope for revolution may be with them
18. A vocabulary consists of everyday ____
20. Author of 1984
22. Freedom is ___
23. Contains the history of the Party & the Brotherhood; The ___
24. Mood of the novel
28. Group frenzy agains the Brotherhood; Two Minutes ____

1984 UNIT CROSSWORD 3

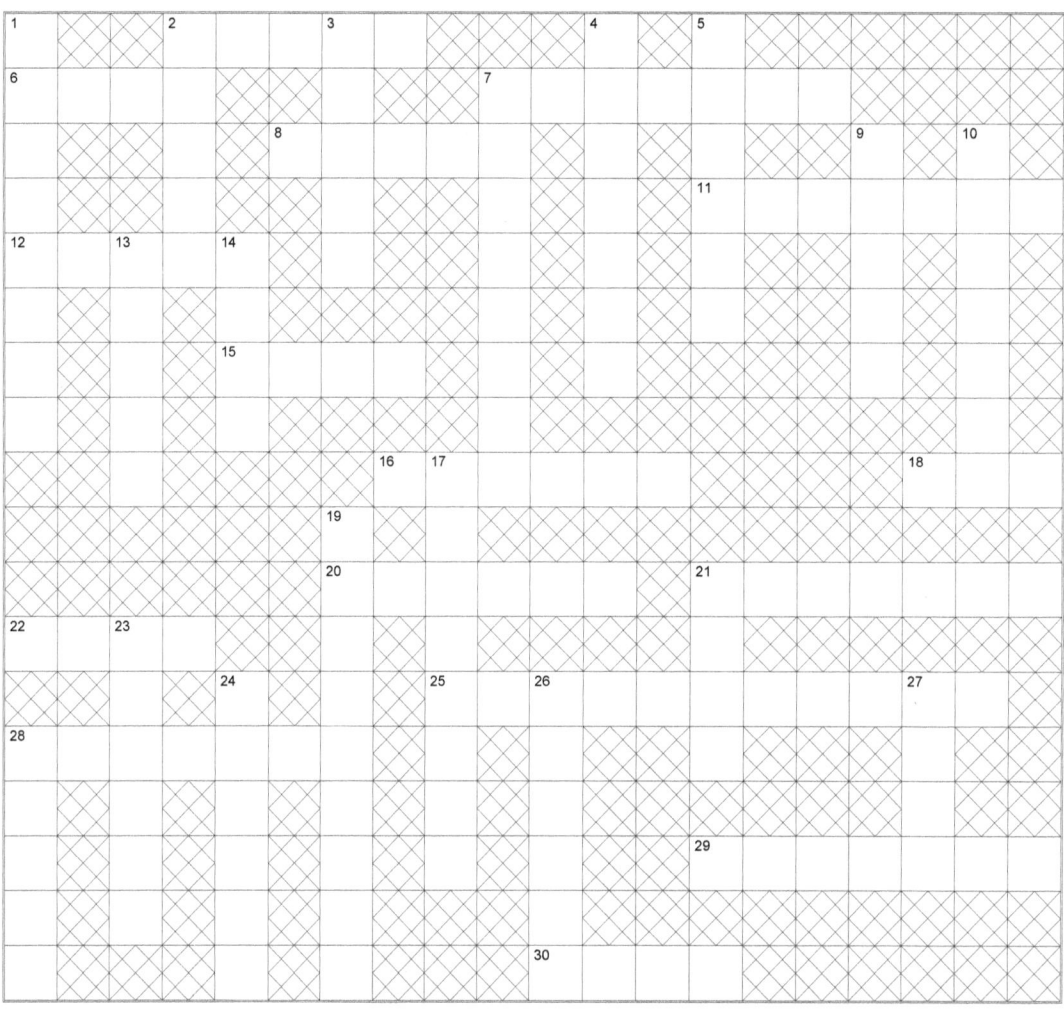

Across
2. Rewriting and distorting history was ___'s job
6. Maintains law and order; Ministry of ___
7. He doesn't believe in the Party doctrine
8. Hates the Party but participates enthusiastically
11. Ministry of Love in Newspeak
12. Ultimate goal of the Party
15. Winston knew 2+2=4 was ___
16. English socialism; philosophy of the Party
18. Aim is to use products but not raise standard of living
20. Author of 1984
21. Not allowed by the Party
22. Contains the history of the Party & the Brotherhood; The ___
25. Winston bought it; it is destroyed when he is captured
28. He is denounced by his daughter
29. Freedom is ___
30. Writing the 11th Edition of the Newspeak dictionary is ___'s job

Down
1. Language that is gradually being replaced
2. Common ___ was the heresy of heresies
3. Responsible for news, entertainment, education, arts; Ministry of ___
4. Winston and Julia meet in its upstairs room; ___ shop
5. Real concept from the 1960's connected to the novel; ___ war
7. Big Brother is _____ you
9. April 4, 1984 is the day Winston starts his ___
10. Enemy superstate as novel opens
13. A vocabulary consists of everyday ___
14. Winston's main fear and eventually his breaking point
17. Language that narrows the range of thought
19. Enemy of the People; image used to create hatred; Emmanuel ___
21. Winston's diary entry: ___ with Big Brother
23. Re-educated Winston; wrote part of The Book
24. Setting of the novel
26. Only hope for revolution may be with them
27. Group frenzy agains the Brotherhood; Two Minutes ___
28. Responsible for war related events; Ministry of ___

1984 UNIT CROSSWORD 3 KEY

Across
- 2. Rewriting and distorting history was ___'s job
- 6. Maintains law and order; Ministry of ___
- 7. He doesn't believe in the Party doctrine
- 8. Hates the Party but participates enthusiastically
- 11. Ministry of Love in Newspeak
- 12. Ultimate goal of the Party
- 15. Winston knew 2+2=4 was ___
- 16. English socialism; philosophy of the Party
- 18. Aim is to use products but not raise standard of living
- 20. Author of 1984
- 21. Not allowed by the Party
- 22. Contains the history of the Party & the Brotherhood; The ___
- 25. Winston bought it; it is destroyed when he is captured
- 28. He is denounced by his daughter
- 29. Freedom is ___
- 30. Writing the 11th Edition of the Newspeak dictionary is ___'s job

Down
- 1. Language that is gradually being replaced
- 2. Common ___ was the heresy of heresies
- 3. Responsible for news, entertainment, education, arts; Ministry of ___
- 4. Winston and Julia meet in its upstairs room; ___ shop
- 5. Real concept from the 1960's connected to the novel; ___ war
- 7. Big Brother is _____ you
- 9. April 4, 1984 is the day Winston starts his ___
- 10. Enemy superstate as novel opens
- 13. A vocabulary consists of everyday ____
- 14. Winston's main fear and eventually his breaking point
- 17. Language that narrows the range of thought
- 19. Enemy of the People; image used to create hatred; Emmanuel ___
- 21. Winston's diary entry: ___ with Big Brother
- 23. Re-educated Winston; wrote part of The Book
- 24. Setting of the novel
- 26. Only hope for revolution may be with them
- 27. Group frenzy agains the Brotherhood; Two Minutes ____
- 28. Responsible for war related events; Ministry of ___

1984 UNIT CROSSWORD 4

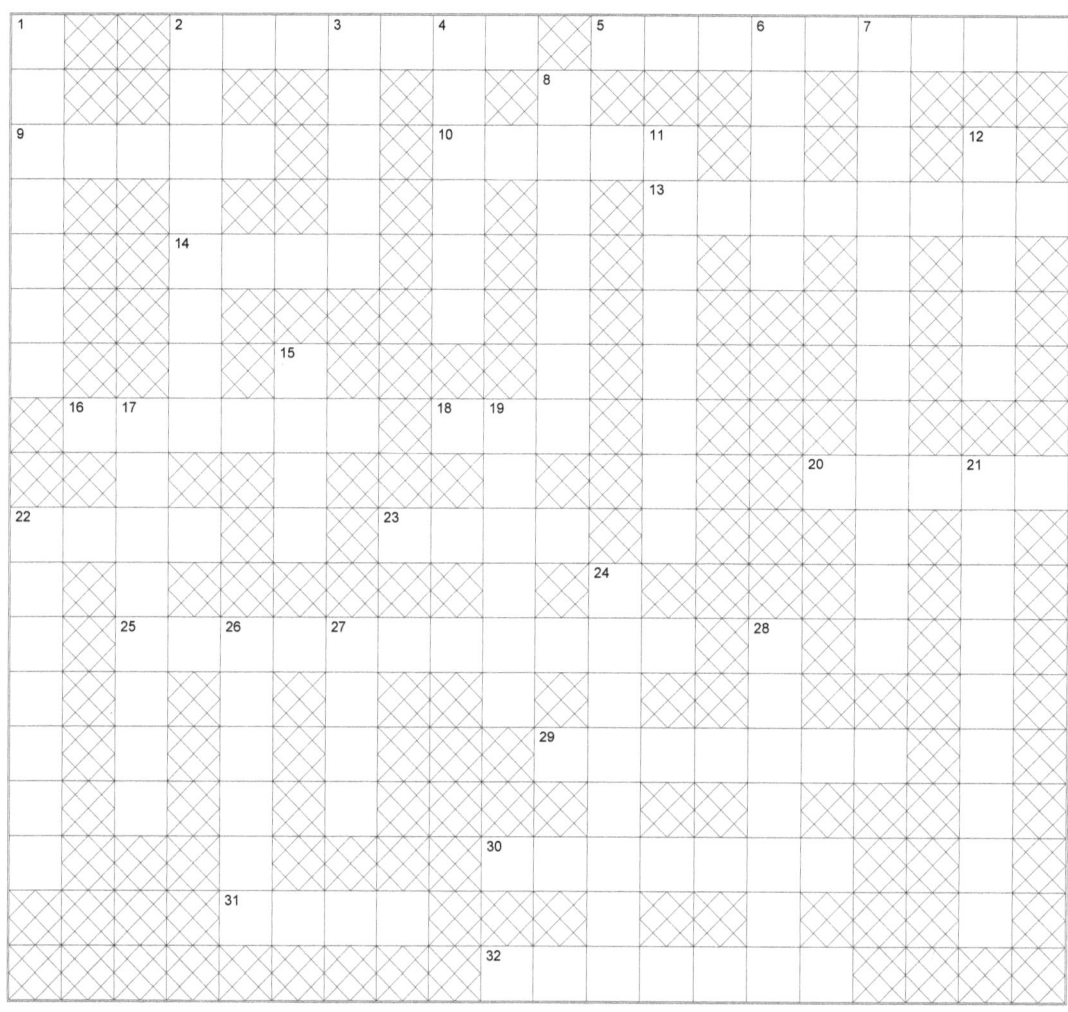

Across
2. He doesn't believe in the Party doctrine
5. Enemy of the People; image used to create hatred; Emmanuel ___
9. Rewriting and distorting history was ___'s job
10. A vocabulary consists of everyday ___
13. O'Brien ___ Winston until he believed 2+2=5
14. Group frenzy agains the Brotherhood; Two Minutes ___
16. English socialism; philosophy of the Party
18. Aim is to use products but not raise standard of living
20. Responsible for news, entertainment, education, arts; Ministry of ___
22. Winston's diary entry: ___ with Big Brother
23. Contains the history of the Party & the Brotherhood; The ___
25. Winston bought it; it is destroyed when he is captured
29. Freedom is ___
30. He is denounced by his daughter
31. Writing the 11th Edition of the Newspeak dictionary is ___'s job
32. Ministry of Peace in Newspeak

Down
1. Mood of the novel
2. Big Brother is ___ you
3. Common ___ was the heresy of heresies
4. Author of 1984
6. April 4, 1984 is the day Winston starts his ___
7. Thinking that is not allowed
8. Head of the Party; Big ___
11. Ignorance is ___
12. Responsible for war related events; Ministry of ___
15. Maintains law and order; Ministry of ___
17. Language that narrows the range of thought
19. Real concept from the 1960's connected to the novel; ___ war
21. C vocabulary consists of words used in ___ fields
22. Not allowed by the Party
24. Taught at school to spy on parents & others
26. Only hope for revolution may be with them
27. Winston's main fear and eventually his breaking point
28. Superstate ruled by the Party

1984 UNIT CROSSWORD 4 KEY

Across
2. He doesn't believe in the Party doctrine
5. Enemy of the People; image used to create hatred; Emmanuel ___
9. Rewriting and distorting history was ___'s job
10. A vocabulary consists of everyday ___
13. O'Brien ___ Winston until he believed 2+2=5
14. Group frenzy agains the Brotherhood; Two Minutes ___
16. English socialism; philosophy of the Party
18. Aim is to use products but not raise standard of living
20. Responsible for news, entertainment, education, arts; Ministry of ___
22. Winston's diary entry: ___ with Big Brother
23. Contains the history of the Party & the Brotherhood; The ___
25. Winston bought it; it is destroyed when he is captured
29. Freedom is ___
30. He is denounced by his daughter
31. Writing the 11th Edition of the Newspeak dictionary is ___'s job
32. Ministry of Peace in Newspeak

Down
1. Mood of the novel
2. Big Brother is ___ you
3. Common ___ was the heresy of heresies
4. Author of 1984
6. April 4, 1984 is the day Winston starts his ___
7. Thinking that is not allowed
8. Head of the Party; Big ___
11. Ignorance is ___
12. Responsible for war related events; Ministry of ___
15. Maintains law and order; Ministry of ___
17. Language that narrows the range of thought
19. Real concept from the 1960's connected to the novel; ___ war
21. C vocabulary consists of words used in ___ fields
22. Not allowed by the Party
24. Taught at school to spy on parents & others
26. Only hope for revolution may be with them
27. Winston's main fear and eventually his breaking point
28. Superstate ruled by the Party

1984 UNIT BINGO CARDS

ANTIQUE	DIARY	SLAVERY	TORTURED	MINIPLENTY
STRENGTH	POLITICAL	BOOK	WINSTON	DIVORCE
BROTHERHOOD	NEWSPEAK	FREE SPACE	TRUE	FACECRIME
POWER	SMITH	PEACE	CHILDREN	DUCKSPEAK
THOUGHTCRIME	SLOGAN	RATS	TRUTH	TELESCREEN

DESPAIR	SENSE	DOWN	ATOMIC	WAR
LOVE	DOUBLETHINK	BROTHER	OCEANIA	AMPLEFORTH
PROLES	MINIPAX	FREE SPACE	REINTEGRATION	SCIENCE
JULIA	THOUGHT	ORWELL	EASTASIA	SYME
OBRIEN	OLDSPEAK	PARSONS	MINILUV	GOLDSTEIN

1984

PROLES	THOUGHTCRIME	SENSE	WAR	WORDS
TORTURED	SCIENCE	JULIA	CHARRINGTON	CHILDREN
TELESCREEN	DOUBLETHINK	FREE SPACE	ATOMIC	POWER
STRENGTH	MINILUV	DOWN	WINSTON	NEWSPEAK
ORWELL	SLOGAN	BROTHERHOOD	BOOK	BROTHER

1984

THOUGHT	REINTEGRATION	OCEANIA	FACECRIME	OLDSPEAK
DIARY	MINITRUE	RATS	SYME	TECHNICAL
OBRIEN	EURASIA	FREE SPACE	INGSOC	MINIPAX
PARSONS	POLITICAL	PEACE	SMITH	AMPLEFORTH
DIVORCE	PAPERWEIGHT	MINIPLENTY	SLAVERY	TRUTH

1984

TRUTH	TELESCREEN	WINSTON	TECHNICAL	OBRIEN
TORTURED	HATE	EASTASIA	ANTIQUE	THOUGHTCRIME
POWER	ORWELL	FREE SPACE	DOUBLETHINK	CHARRINGTON
MINITRUE	BROTHER	SMITH	OLDSPEAK	SLOGAN
NEWSPEAK	PROLES	WAR	PLENTY	SENSE

1984

DIARY	STRENGTH	LONDON	CHILDREN	TRUE
RATS	WORDS	MINIPLENTY	INGSOC	DUCKSPEAK
JULIA	AMPLEFORTH	FREE SPACE	PEACE	WATCHING
SYME	EURASIA	OCEANIA	POLITICAL	PARSONS
PAPERWEIGHT	THOUGHT	BOOK	REINTEGRATION	BROTHERHOOD

1984

STRENGTH	ATOMIC	SLAVERY	OBRIEN	MINIPAX
DUCKSPEAK	TRUTH	JULIA	DESPAIR	NEWSPEAK
MINILUV	BROTHERHOOD	FREE SPACE	ANTIQUE	PLENTY
RATS	SYME	TRUE	PROLES	DOWN
SCIENCE	SLOGAN	PEACE	PAPERWEIGHT	MINITRUE

1984

OCEANIA	SMITH	REINTEGRATION	WAR	DIARY
DOUBLETHINK	AMPLEFORTH	GOLDSTEIN	WATCHING	LONDON
BROTHER	INGSOC	FREE SPACE	TORTURED	DIVORCE
EASTASIA	ORWELL	CHILDREN	WORDS	POWER
EURASIA	SENSE	TELESCREEN	FACECRIME	HATE

1984

TRUE	PARSONS	DOUBLETHINK	MINITRUE	STRENGTH
BOOK	POLITICAL	MINIPAX	EURASIA	THOUGHT
PEACE	SCIENCE	FREE SPACE	LOVE	TECHNICAL
REINTEGRATION	GOLDSTEIN	WATCHING	BROTHERHOOD	CHILDREN
WINSTON	TRUTH	MINILUV	NEWSPEAK	POWER

1984

THOUGHTCRIME	FACECRIME	MINIPLENTY	OBRIEN	RATS
PLENTY	DIARY	SLAVERY	ORWELL	EASTASIA
SMITH	PROLES	FREE SPACE	TORTURED	SLOGAN
INGSOC	ATOMIC	ANTIQUE	BROTHER	OLDSPEAK
DUCKSPEAK	SENSE	SYME	HATE	PAPERWEIGHT

1984

INGSOC	DUCKSPEAK	THOUGHTCRIME	LOVE	SCIENCE
DESPAIR	EASTASIA	MINIPAX	PEACE	OLDSPEAK
NEWSPEAK	POLITICAL	FREE SPACE	TORTURED	DOUBLETHINK
OCEANIA	CHILDREN	ATOMIC	CHARRINGTON	TELESCREEN
BROTHERHOOD	PARSONS	DIARY	SLOGAN	JULIA

1984

GOLDSTEIN	PAPERWEIGHT	TRUE	BOOK	HATE
ORWELL	WINSTON	SMITH	FACECRIME	TECHNICAL
ANTIQUE	STRENGTH	FREE SPACE	MINIPLENTY	TRUTH
EURASIA	WATCHING	RATS	MINITRUE	WAR
PLENTY	SLAVERY	PROLES	LONDON	BROTHER

1984

ATOMIC	DIARY	TRUTH	AMPLEFORTH	SMITH
PARSONS	THOUGHTCRIME	MINIPLENTY	DUCKSPEAK	ORWELL
POLITICAL	WATCHING	FREE SPACE	EURASIA	WORDS
GOLDSTEIN	HATE	PLENTY	BROTHERHOOD	LOVE
CHILDREN	TORTURED	NEWSPEAK	OLDSPEAK	OBRIEN

1984

MINILUV	EASTASIA	BOOK	MINITRUE	SLAVERY
RATS	WAR	THOUGHT	TECHNICAL	CHARRINGTON
REINTEGRATION	OCEANIA	FREE SPACE	WINSTON	PROLES
STRENGTH	SLOGAN	PEACE	SENSE	SYME
INGSOC	DESPAIR	POWER	TRUE	DIVORCE

1984

SENSE	LOVE	TELESCREEN	TECHNICAL	TRUE
GOLDSTEIN	THOUGHT	NEWSPEAK	MINIPAX	SYME
THOUGHTCRIME	OLDSPEAK	FREE SPACE	BOOK	MINITRUE
SLAVERY	HATE	STRENGTH	SMITH	POLITICAL
DOUBLETHINK	TORTURED	PEACE	REINTEGRATION	WINSTON

1984

EURASIA	DOWN	MINILUV	ORWELL	PARSONS
TRUTH	RATS	CHILDREN	PLENTY	DUCKSPEAK
CHARRINGTON	JULIA	FREE SPACE	POWER	BROTHERHOOD
ATOMIC	EASTASIA	WAR	LONDON	OCEANIA
INGSOC	BROTHER	FACECRIME	AMPLEFORTH	ANTIQUE

1984

WATCHING	LOVE	SENSE	TRUTH	FACECRIME
GOLDSTEIN	THOUGHTCRIME	OLDSPEAK	MINILUV	REINTEGRATION
MINIPLENTY	PROLES	FREE SPACE	ANTIQUE	EURASIA
POLITICAL	SLOGAN	PLENTY	THOUGHT	ATOMIC
LONDON	BOOK	STRENGTH	DIARY	TORTURED

1984

WORDS	TELESCREEN	POWER	PAPERWEIGHT	WINSTON
TECHNICAL	CHILDREN	MINIPAX	EASTASIA	SCIENCE
RATS	BROTHER	FREE SPACE	OBRIEN	PARSONS
ORWELL	AMPLEFORTH	SMITH	DOUBLETHINK	INGSOC
SLAVERY	HATE	OCEANIA	NEWSPEAK	DIVORCE

1984

MINITRUE	GOLDSTEIN	PROLES	AMPLEFORTH	OBRIEN
BOOK	ANTIQUE	LONDON	PEACE	PAPERWEIGHT
THOUGHTCRIME	DOWN	FREE SPACE	WINSTON	HATE
MINIPAX	CHILDREN	SLAVERY	LOVE	OLDSPEAK
DIARY	WATCHING	TECHNICAL	CHARRINGTON	PARSONS

1984

BROTHER	DESPAIR	STRENGTH	INGSOC	POLITICAL
TORTURED	SLOGAN	OCEANIA	WAR	SCIENCE
ATOMIC	EURASIA	FREE SPACE	REINTEGRATION	DUCKSPEAK
DIVORCE	SYME	WORDS	SMITH	RATS
PLENTY	TRUTH	ORWELL	POWER	EASTASIA

1984

MINITRUE	PARSONS	DESPAIR	FACECRIME	MINIPAX
JULIA	TECHNICAL	PAPERWEIGHT	TELESCREEN	PEACE
CHILDREN	SYME	FREE SPACE	MINILUV	DUCKSPEAK
WAR	SMITH	NEWSPEAK	ORWELL	OLDSPEAK
DOUBLETHINK	TRUE	RATS	POWER	SCIENCE

1984

THOUGHTCRIME	STRENGTH	PLENTY	ANTIQUE	PROLES
EASTASIA	AMPLEFORTH	LOVE	MINIPLENTY	WATCHING
TORTURED	TRUTH	FREE SPACE	WORDS	BROTHERHOOD
THOUGHT	GOLDSTEIN	OBRIEN	DIVORCE	POLITICAL
REINTEGRATION	SLOGAN	EURASIA	ATOMIC	HATE

1984

TELESCREEN	DIARY	CHARRINGTON	CHILDREN	TRUTH
JULIA	REINTEGRATION	ORWELL	OLDSPEAK	DIVORCE
LONDON	PEACE	FREE SPACE	MINILUV	EURASIA
DESPAIR	WAR	SLAVERY	SYME	PARSONS
SMITH	PLENTY	BROTHER	LOVE	SENSE

1984

ANTIQUE	WINSTON	PROLES	MINIPAX	STRENGTH
SLOGAN	DOWN	BROTHERHOOD	TRUE	AMPLEFORTH
NEWSPEAK	INGSOC	FREE SPACE	ATOMIC	WATCHING
PAPERWEIGHT	POLITICAL	THOUGHT	GOLDSTEIN	TORTURED
MINIPLENTY	RATS	MINITRUE	POWER	SCIENCE

1984

PARSONS	WATCHING	ATOMIC	FACECRIME	POWER
NEWSPEAK	OBRIEN	PLENTY	GOLDSTEIN	PROLES
MINILUV	MINIPLENTY	FREE SPACE	WAR	DESPAIR
MINITRUE	CHARRINGTON	ANTIQUE	TECHNICAL	REINTEGRATION
THOUGHTCRIME	EURASIA	SMITH	MINIPAX	SYME

1984

HATE	OLDSPEAK	AMPLEFORTH	TRUTH	TORTURED
OCEANIA	ORWELL	WORDS	BOOK	CHILDREN
DIVORCE	BROTHER	FREE SPACE	DOUBLETHINK	DOWN
DIARY	DUCKSPEAK	LOVE	RATS	POLITICAL
JULIA	TELESCREEN	THOUGHT	SLOGAN	TRUE

1984

AMPLEFORTH	POWER	FACECRIME	BOOK	SLAVERY
ORWELL	ANTIQUE	PARSONS	TRUE	THOUGHT
MINITRUE	SCIENCE	FREE SPACE	MINIPAX	DESPAIR
DOWN	BROTHER	MINIPLENTY	CHILDREN	ATOMIC
MINILUV	THOUGHTCRIME	DIARY	HATE	BROTHERHOOD

1984

WINSTON	PEACE	WORDS	RATS	SENSE
WAR	TELESCREEN	WATCHING	DUCKSPEAK	SLOGAN
OBRIEN	PROLES	FREE SPACE	NEWSPEAK	INGSOC
PLENTY	SYME	OCEANIA	TECHNICAL	POLITICAL
LOVE	CHARRINGTON	GOLDSTEIN	DOUBLETHINK	JULIA

1984

AMPLEFORTH	TECHNICAL	THOUGHTCRIME	EURASIA	SLAVERY
PAPERWEIGHT	BOOK	MINILUV	PLENTY	HATE
MINITRUE	LOVE	FREE SPACE	EASTASIA	MINIPAX
CHARRINGTON	TRUTH	GOLDSTEIN	OCEANIA	PEACE
POLITICAL	DOWN	PARSONS	DUCKSPEAK	MINIPLENTY

1984

ANTIQUE	SMITH	DIARY	SYME	CHILDREN
ORWELL	SCIENCE	OLDSPEAK	POWER	RATS
OBRIEN	PROLES	FREE SPACE	STRENGTH	WINSTON
WORDS	WAR	BROTHER	DESPAIR	LONDON
FACECRIME	NEWSPEAK	JULIA	DIVORCE	DOUBLETHINK

1984

WAR	HATE	RATS	CHILDREN	DOUBLETHINK
CHARRINGTON	LOVE	AMPLEFORTH	PROLES	MINITRUE
ORWELL	EASTASIA	FREE SPACE	TRUTH	SENSE
SLAVERY	PLENTY	DUCKSPEAK	SCIENCE	EURASIA
TRUE	TECHNICAL	BROTHER	SYME	WATCHING

1984

OLDSPEAK	OBRIEN	PEACE	NEWSPEAK	LONDON
TORTURED	BROTHERHOOD	INGSOC	THOUGHT	WORDS
PAPERWEIGHT	POLITICAL	FREE SPACE	PARSONS	MINILUV
BOOK	POWER	GOLDSTEIN	MINIPAX	WINSTON
DIVORCE	TELESCREEN	OCEANIA	DIARY	DESPAIR

1984 Vocabulary Word List

No.	Word	Clue/Definition
1.	ABASHED	Embarrassed
2.	ABSURDITY	Nonsense
3.	ABYSS	Lowest depth
4.	ACCUMULATED	Collected
5.	ARBITRARY	Without regard to a rule or law
6.	ATROCITY	Extreme wickedness or cruelty
7.	AXIOM	Statement taken to be true without proof
8.	BIGOTED	Unreasonably attached to an opinion or belief
9.	CALLOUSNESS	An unfeeling manner; hard-heartedness
10.	CAPITALISTS	People who use money to carry on business
11.	CAPITULATED	Gave up
12.	CLANDESTINELY	Done in a secret or underhanded manner
13.	COMMOTION	Excited noise and activity
14.	CONSUMPTION	Things made to be used up
15.	CONTRIVED	Planned; designed
16.	CONVOLUTED	Having folds or winding curves
17.	CULPABLE	Deserving blame
18.	DEGRADATION	Worn or broken down condition
19.	DEMEANOR	Behavior; manner
20.	DESULTORILY	Jumping from one topic to another
21.	DIMINUTION	Reduction; decrease
22.	EMACIATION	Losing flesh; wasting away
23.	EMPIRICAL	Based on experiment and observation
24.	ENVELOPING	Surrounding
25.	EQUIVOCATION	Not making a commitment on a matter
26.	ERADICATE	Destroy; wipe out
27.	EUPHEMISMS	Mild or indirect expressions
28.	EUPHONY	Combination of pleasant sounds
29.	EXTRICATE	Set free; release
30.	FATUOUS	Silly; foolish
31.	HIERARCHIAL	Arranging things one above the other by rank
32.	IDEOLOGICAL	Having to do with the opinions of a person or political movement
33.	IMPENDING	About to happen
34.	IMPREGNABLE	Won't give in to force or persuasion
35.	INCREDULITY	Lack of belief
36.	INCREDULOUS	Not believing
37.	INCRIMINATING	Showing guilt
38.	INDIGNATION	Anger combined with disapproval
39.	INDOCTRINATE	Teach a belief or principal
40.	INEXORABLY	Relentlessly; unyielding
41.	INFALLIBLE	Free from error
42.	INIMICAL	Harmful; unfavorable
43.	INIQUITY	Wickedness
44.	INSTALLMENTS	Parts of a series
45.	INTEGRITY	Honesty; sincerity
46.	INTIMIDATING	Frightening
47.	INTOLERABLE	Too much to be endured
48.	INVIOLATE	Unbroken; uninjured
49.	IRONICAL	Expressing one thing and meaning another
50.	IRRECONCILABLE	Not able to agree
51.	JARGON	Language of a special group

1984 Vocabulary Word List

No. Word	Clue/Definition
52. LETHARGY	Drowsy dullness or lack of activity
53. LUMINOUS	Shining by its own light
54. MALLEABLE	Able to be shaped or molded
55. METAPHYSICS	An attempt to explain reality and knowledge
56. OLIGARCHIES	Governments ruled by only a few people
57. OMNIPOTENT	Having great power or influence
58. ORIFICES	Openings; holes
59. PALPABLE	Easily seen or heard and recognized
60. PERCEPTIBLE	Observable; understandable
61. PERSIFLAGE	Joking talk or writing
62. POSTERITY	Future generations
63. PRAGMATISM	Judging things on their practical consequences
64. PRECISION	Accuracy; exactness
65. PRODIGIES	Marvelous examples
66. PROLETARIAT	The lowest economic or social class
67. PROSTRATED	Lying down flat
68. PURGES	Removal of undesirable people from a nation or party
69. RAMIFICATIONS	Branches; subdivisions
70. RASH	Hasty and careless
71. RECONCILIATION	Bringing together again in friendship
72. SABOTAGE	Damage or destruction done as an attack
73. SCRUTINIZED	Examined carefully
74. SERVILE	Giving in because of fear
75. SINECURES	Very easy jobs that pay well
76. SMUGLY	In a way that is too pleased with oneself
77. SOCIALISM	Government production and distribution of goods
78. SPURIOUS	False; not genuine
79. STRIDENT	Having a harsh sound
80. SUBSIDIARY	Secondary
81. SUCCUMBED	Gave way; yielded
82. SUPERFLUOUS	Unnecessary
83. TACITLY	Understood without being openly said
84. TORPID	Dull; inactive
85. UNDECIPHERABLE	Not clear
86. UNORTHODOXY	Not holding generally accepted beliefs
87. VAGUE	Not definite or precise
88. VINDICATE	Excuse; absolve
89. ZEALOT	Person who shows too much enthusiasm; a fanatic

1984 VOCABULARY FILL IN THE BLANK 1

_____ 1. Dull; inactive

_____ 2. Collected

_____ 3. Judging things on their practical consequences

_____ 4. Set free; release

_____ 5. Openings; holes

_____ 6. Hasty and careless

_____ 7. Having to do with the opinions of a person or political movement

_____ 8. Easily seen or heard and recognized

_____ 9. Arranging things one above the other by rank

_____ 10. Unreasonably attached to an opinion or belief

_____ 11. Having a harsh sound

_____ 12. Government production and distribution of goods

_____ 13. Understood without being openly said

_____ 14. Bringing together again in friendship

_____ 15. Excuse; absolve

_____ 16. Marvelous examples

_____ 17. Secondary

_____ 18. The lowest economic or social class

_____ 19. Nonsense

_____ 20. Able to be shaped or molded

1984 VOCABULARY FILL IN THE BLANK 1 KEY

TORPID	1. Dull; inactive
ACCUMULATED	2. Collected
PRAGMATISM	3. Judging things on their practical consequences
EXTRICATE	4. Set free; release
ORIFICES	5. Openings; holes
RASH	6. Hasty and careless
IDEOLOGICAL	7. Having to do with the opinions of a person or political movement
PALPABLE	8. Easily seen or heard and recognized
HIERARCHIAL	9. Arranging things one above the other by rank
BIGOTED	10. Unreasonably attached to an opinion or belief
STRIDENT	11. Having a harsh sound
SOCIALISM	12. Government production and distribution of goods
TACITLY	13. Understood without being openly said
RECONCILIATION	14. Bringing together again in friendship
VINDICATE	15. Excuse; absolve
PRODIGIES	16. Marvelous examples
SUBSIDIARY	17. Secondary
PROLETARIAT	18. The lowest economic or social class
ABSURDITY	19. Nonsense
MALLEABLE	20. Able to be shaped or molded

1984 VOCABULARY FILL IN THE BLANK 2

1. Excuse; absolve
2. Government production and distribution of goods
3. Things made to be used up
4. Combination of pleasant sounds
5. Destroy; wipe out
6. Having to do with the opinions of a person or political movement
7. Examined carefully
8. Embarrassed
9. Shining by its own light
10. Unreasonably attached to an opinion or belief
11. Removal of undesirable people from a nation or party
12. An attempt to explain reality and knowledge
13. Not believing
14. Observable; understandable
15. Won't give in to force or persuasion
16. Unbroken; uninjured
17. Based on experiment and observation
18. In a way that is too pleased with oneself
19. Accuracy; exactness
20. Surrounding

1984 VOCABULARY FILL IN THE BLANK 2 KEY

VINDICATE	1. Excuse; absolve
SOCIALISM	2. Government production and distribution of goods
CONSUMPTION	3. Things made to be used up
EUPHONY	4. Combination of pleasant sounds
ERADICATE	5. Destroy; wipe out
IDEOLOGICAL	6. Having to do with the opinions of a person or political movement
SCRUTINIZED	7. Examined carefully
ABASHED	8. Embarrassed
LUMINOUS	9. Shining by its own light
BIGOTED	10. Unreasonably attached to an opinion or belief
PURGES	11. Removal of undesirable people from a nation or party
METAPHYSICS	12. An attempt to explain reality and knowledge
INCREDULOUS	13. Not believing
PERCEPTIBLE	14. Observable; understandable
IMPREGNABLE	15. Won't give in to force or persuasion
INVIOLATE	16. Unbroken; uninjured
EMPIRICAL	17. Based on experiment and observation
SMUGLY	18. In a way that is too pleased with oneself
PRECISION	19. Accuracy; exactness
ENVELOPING	20. Surrounding

Copyrighted Materials

1984 VOCABULARY FILL IN THE BLANK 3

_____   1. Examined carefully

_____   2. Having folds or winding curves

_____   3. Based on experiment and observation

_____   4. Damage or destruction done as an attack

_____   5. Things made to be used up

_____   6. Joking talk or writing

_____   7. Not definite or precise

_____   8. An unfeeling manner; hard-heartedness

_____   9. Deserving blame

_____   10. Marvelous examples

_____   11. Understood without being openly said

_____   12. Planned; designed

_____   13. Secondary

_____   14. Removal of undesirable people from a nation or party

_____   15. Easily seen or heard and recognized

_____   16. Mild or indirect expressions

_____   17. Future generations

_____   18. Lack of belief

_____   19. Judging things on their practical consequences

_____   20. Government production and distribution of goods

1984 VOCABULARY FILL IN THE BLANK 3 KEY

SCRUTINIZED	1. Examined carefully
CONVOLUTED	2. Having folds or winding curves
EMPIRICAL	3. Based on experiment and observation
SABOTAGE	4. Damage or destruction done as an attack
CONSUMPTION	5. Things made to be used up
PERSIFLAGE	6. Joking talk or writing
VAGUE	7. Not definite or precise
CALLOUSNESS	8. An unfeeling manner; hard-heartedness
CULPABLE	9. Deserving blame
PRODIGIES	10. Marvelous examples
TACITLY	11. Understood without being openly said
CONTRIVED	12. Planned; designed
SUBSIDIARY	13. Secondary
PURGES	14. Removal of undesirable people from a nation or party
PALPABLE	15. Easily seen or heard and recognized
EUPHEMISMS	16. Mild or indirect expressions
POSTERITY	17. Future generations
INCREDULITY	18. Lack of belief
PRAGMATISM	19. Judging things on their practical consequences
SOCIALISM	20. Government production and distribution of goods

Copyrighted Materials

1984 VOCABULARY FILL IN THE BLANK 4

_____   1. Able to be shaped or molded

_____   2. Teach a belief or principal

_____   3. Gave up

_____   4. Worn or broken down condition

_____   5. Collected

_____   6. Embarrassed

_____   7. Easily seen or heard and recognized

_____   8. Very easy jobs that pay well

_____   9. Drowsy dullness or lack of activity

_____   10. Without regard to a rule or law

_____   11. Accuracy; exactness

_____   12. Reduction; decrease

_____   13. Examined carefully

_____   14. Excited noise and activity

_____   15. Branches; subdivisions

_____   16. Not making a commitment on a matter

_____   17. Statement taken to be true without proof

_____   18. Behavior; manner

_____   19. Too much to be endured

_____   20. Gave way; yielded

1984 VOCABULARY FILL IN THE BLANK 4 KEY

MALLEABLE	1. Able to be shaped or molded
INDOCTRINATE	2. Teach a belief or principal
CAPITULATED	3. Gave up
DEGRADATION	4. Worn or broken down condition
ACCUMULATED	5. Collected
ABASHED	6. Embarrassed
PALPABLE	7. Easily seen or heard and recognized
SINECURES	8. Very easy jobs that pay well
LETHARGY	9. Drowsy dullness or lack of activity
ARBITRARY	10. Without regard to a rule or law
PRECISION	11. Accuracy; exactness
DIMINUTION	12. Reduction; decrease
SCRUTINIZED	13. Examined carefully
COMMOTION	14. Excited noise and activity
RAMIFICATIONS	15. Branches; subdivisions
EQUIVOCATION	16. Not making a commitment on a matter
AXIOM	17. Statement taken to be true without proof
DEMEANOR	18. Behavior; manner
INTOLERABLE	19. Too much to be endured
SUCCUMBED	20. Gave way; yielded

1984 VOCABULARY MATCHING 1

___ 1. LETHARGY   A. An unfeeling manner; hard-heartedness
___ 2. ENVELOPING   B. Language of a special group
___ 3. UNORTHODOXY   C. Surrounding
___ 4. ZEALOT   D. Deserving blame
___ 5. LUMINOUS   E. Excuse; absolve
___ 6. ERADICATE   F. Jumping from one topic to another
___ 7. CONSUMPTION   G. Based on experiment and observation
___ 8. EMPIRICAL   H. Things made to be used up
___ 9. MALLEABLE   I. Unbroken; uninjured
___10. INVIOLATE   J. Nonsense
___11. STRIDENT   K. Shining by its own light
___12. JARGON   L. Not clear
___13. CALLOUSNESS   M. Destroy; wipe out
___14. POSTERITY   N. Having a harsh sound
___15. DIMINUTION   O. About to happen
___16. VINDICATE   P. Expressing one thing and meaning another
___17. PRECISION   Q. Openings; holes
___18. ABSURDITY   R. Person who shows too much enthusiasm; a fanatic
___19. ORIFICES   S. Not holding generally accepted beliefs
___20. UNDECIPHERABLE   T. Teach a belief or principal
___21. INDOCTRINATE   U. Able to be shaped or molded
___22. IRONICAL   V. Future generations
___23. IMPENDING   W. Drowsy dullness or lack of activity
___24. CULPABLE   X. Accuracy; exactness
___25. DESULTORILY   Y. Reduction; decrease

1984 VOCABULARY MATCHING 1 KEY

W - 1. LETHARGY	A.	An unfeeling manner; hard-heartedness
C - 2. ENVELOPING	B.	Language of a special group
S - 3. UNORTHODOXY	C.	Surrounding
R - 4. ZEALOT	D.	Deserving blame
K - 5. LUMINOUS	E.	Excuse; absolve
M - 6. ERADICATE	F.	Jumping from one topic to another
H - 7. CONSUMPTION	G.	Based on experiment and observation
G - 8. EMPIRICAL	H.	Things made to be used up
U - 9. MALLEABLE	I.	Unbroken; uninjured
I - 10. INVIOLATE	J.	Nonsense
N - 11. STRIDENT	K.	Shining by its own light
B - 12. JARGON	L.	Not clear
A - 13. CALLOUSNESS	M.	Destroy; wipe out
V - 14. POSTERITY	N.	Having a harsh sound
Y - 15. DIMINUTION	O.	About to happen
E - 16. VINDICATE	P.	Expressing one thing and meaning another
X - 17. PRECISION	Q.	Openings; holes
J - 18. ABSURDITY	R.	Person who shows too much enthusiasm; a fanatic
Q - 19. ORIFICES	S.	Not holding generally accepted beliefs
L - 20. UNDECIPHERABLE	T.	Teach a belief or principal
T - 21. INDOCTRINATE	U.	Able to be shaped or molded
P - 22. IRONICAL	V.	Future generations
O - 23. IMPENDING	W.	Drowsy dullness or lack of activity
D - 24. CULPABLE	X.	Accuracy; exactness
F - 25. DESULTORILY	Y.	Reduction; decrease

1984 VOCABULARY MATCHING 2

___ 1. PRAGMATISM   A. Marvelous examples
___ 2. SABOTAGE   B. Judging things on their practical consequences
___ 3. SINECURES   C. Very easy jobs that pay well
___ 4. INCREDULITY   D. Unbroken; uninjured
___ 5. LETHARGY   E. Not believing
___ 6. PRODIGIES   F. Damage or destruction done as an attack
___ 7. VAGUE   G. Not definite or precise
___ 8. CALLOUSNESS   H. Giving in because of fear
___ 9. OLIGARCHIES   I. Joking talk or writing
___10. ARBITRARY   J. Won't give in to force or persuasion
___11. MALLEABLE   K. Having to do with the opinions of a person or political movement
___12. CAPITALISTS   L. False; not genuine
___13. IMPENDING   M. Drowsy dullness or lack of activity
___14. UNDECIPHERABLE   N. Not clear
___15. LUMINOUS   O. Set free; release
___16. CULPABLE   P. Governments ruled by only a few people
___17. INVIOLATE   Q. About to happen
___18. IMPREGNABLE   R. An unfeeling manner; hard-heartedness
___19. SPURIOUS   S. Shining by its own light
___20. OMNIPOTENT   T. Able to be shaped or molded
___21. IDEOLOGICAL   U. People who use money to carry on business
___22. EXTRICATE   V. Having great power or influence
___23. PERSIFLAGE   W. Deserving blame
___24. SERVILE   X. Lack of belief
___25. INCREDULOUS   Y. Without regard to a rule or law

1984 VOCABULARY MATCHING 2 KEY

B - 1. PRAGMATISM	A.	Marvelous examples
F - 2. SABOTAGE	B.	Judging things on their practical consequences
C - 3. SINECURES	C.	Very easy jobs that pay well
X - 4. INCREDULITY	D.	Unbroken; uninjured
M - 5. LETHARGY	E.	Not believing
A - 6. PRODIGIES	F.	Damage or destruction done as an attack
G - 7. VAGUE	G.	Not definite or precise
R - 8. CALLOUSNESS	H.	Giving in because of fear
P - 9. OLIGARCHIES	I.	Joking talk or writing
Y - 10. ARBITRARY	J.	Won't give in to force or persuasion
T - 11. MALLEABLE	K.	Having to do with the opinions of a person or political movement
U - 12. CAPITALISTS	L.	False; not genuine
Q - 13. IMPENDING	M.	Drowsy dullness or lack of activity
N - 14. UNDECIPHERABLE	N.	Not clear
S - 15. LUMINOUS	O.	Set free; release
W - 16. CULPABLE	P.	Governments ruled by only a few people
D - 17. INVIOLATE	Q.	About to happen
J - 18. IMPREGNABLE	R.	An unfeeling manner; hard-heartedness
L - 19. SPURIOUS	S.	Shining by its own light
V - 20. OMNIPOTENT	T.	Able to be shaped or molded
K - 21. IDEOLOGICAL	U.	People who use money to carry on business
O - 22. EXTRICATE	V.	Having great power or influence
I - 23. PERSIFLAGE	W.	Deserving blame
H - 24. SERVILE	X.	Lack of belief
E - 25. INCREDULOUS	Y.	Without regard to a rule or law

1984 VOCABULARY MATCHING 3

___ 1. INTIMIDATING   A. Marvelous examples
___ 2. PROLETARIAT   B. Shining by its own light
___ 3. JARGON   C. The lowest economic or social class
___ 4. DIMINUTION   D. Planned; designed
___ 5. PRODIGIES   E. Reduction; decrease
___ 6. DEMEANOR   F. Joking talk or writing
___ 7. ENVELOPING   G. Removal of undesirable people from a nation or party
___ 8. FATUOUS   H. Gave way; yielded
___ 9. CONTRIVED   I. Done in a secret or underhanded manner
___10. SUCCUMBED   J. Government production and distribution of goods
___11. CLANDESTINELY   K. Bringing together again in friendship
___12. RECONCILIATION   L. Lack of belief
___13. PERSIFLAGE   M. Behavior; manner
___14. PURGES   N. Very easy jobs that pay well
___15. SOCIALISM   O. Destroy; wipe out
___16. INCREDULITY   P. Mild or indirect expressions
___17. EMACIATION   Q. Losing flesh; wasting away
___18. HIERARCHIAL   R. Frightening
___19. ERADICATE   S. Surrounding
___20. IMPREGNABLE   T. Excited noise and activity
___21. SINECURES   U. Won't give in to force or persuasion
___22. EUPHEMISMS   V. Language of a special group
___23. ABYSS   W. Lowest depth
___24. COMMOTION   X. Arranging things one above the other by rank
___25. LUMINOUS   Y. Silly; foolish

1984 VOCABULARY MATCHING 3 KEY

R - 1. INTIMIDATING A. Marvelous examples
C - 2. PROLETARIAT B. Shining by its own light
V - 3. JARGON C. The lowest economic or social class
E - 4. DIMINUTION D. Planned; designed
A - 5. PRODIGIES E. Reduction; decrease
M - 6. DEMEANOR F. Joking talk or writing
S - 7. ENVELOPING G. Removal of undesirable people from a nation or party
Y - 8. FATUOUS H. Gave way; yielded
D - 9. CONTRIVED I. Done in a secret or underhanded manner
H -10. SUCCUMBED J. Government production and distribution of goods
I -11. CLANDESTINELY K. Bringing together again in friendship
K -12. RECONCILIATION L. Lack of belief
F -13. PERSIFLAGE M. Behavior; manner
G -14. PURGES N. Very easy jobs that pay well
J -15. SOCIALISM O. Destroy; wipe out
L -16. INCREDULITY P. Mild or indirect expressions
Q -17. EMACIATION Q. Losing flesh; wasting away
X -18. HIERARCHIAL R. Frightening
O -19. ERADICATE S. Surrounding
U -20. IMPREGNABLE T. Excited noise and activity
N -21. SINECURES U. Won't give in to force or persuasion
P -22. EUPHEMISMS V. Language of a special group
W -23. ABYSS W. Lowest depth
T -24. COMMOTION X. Arranging things one above the other by rank
B -25. LUMINOUS Y. Silly; foolish

1984 VOCABULARY MATCHING 4

___ 1. ARBITRARY A. Without regard to a rule or law
___ 2. RECONCILIATION B. Having great power or influence
___ 3. TACITLY C. Secondary
___ 4. PERCEPTIBLE D. Marvelous examples
___ 5. COMMOTION E. Honesty; sincerity
___ 6. CULPABLE F. Bringing together again in friendship
___ 7. IMPENDING G. Extreme wickedness or cruelty
___ 8. PROSTRATED H. Losing flesh; wasting away
___ 9. PRAGMATISM I. Not definite or precise
___ 10. VAGUE J. Destroy; wipe out
___ 11. INCRIMINATING K. Showing guilt
___ 12. ORIFICES L. Deserving blame
___ 13. INEXORABLY M. Observable; understandable
___ 14. ABASHED N. Unbroken; uninjured
___ 15. EUPHEMISMS O. Future generations
___ 16. INVIOLATE P. Excited noise and activity
___ 17. PRODIGIES Q. Judging things on their practical consequences
___ 18. INTEGRITY R. Things made to be used up
___ 19. EMACIATION S. Understood without being openly said
___ 20. OMNIPOTENT T. Mild or indirect expressions
___ 21. SUBSIDIARY U. Embarrassed
___ 22. CONSUMPTION V. Relentlessly; unyielding
___ 23. POSTERITY W. Openings; holes
___ 24. ATROCITY X. Lying down flat
___ 25. ERADICATE Y. About to happen

1984 VOCABULARY MATCHING 4 KEY

- A - 1. ARBITRARY
- F - 2. RECONCILIATION
- S - 3. TACITLY
- M - 4. PERCEPTIBLE
- P - 5. COMMOTION
- L - 6. CULPABLE
- Y - 7. IMPENDING
- X - 8. PROSTRATED
- Q - 9. PRAGMATISM
- I - 10. VAGUE
- K - 11. INCRIMINATING
- W - 12. ORIFICES
- V - 13. INEXORABLY
- U - 14. ABASHED
- T - 15. EUPHEMISMS
- N - 16. INVIOLATE
- D - 17. PRODIGIES
- E - 18. INTEGRITY
- H - 19. EMACIATION
- B - 20. OMNIPOTENT
- C - 21. SUBSIDIARY
- R - 22. CONSUMPTION
- O - 23. POSTERITY
- G - 24. ATROCITY
- J - 25. ERADICATE

A. Without regard to a rule or law
B. Having great power or influence
C. Secondary
D. Marvelous examples
E. Honesty; sincerity
F. Bringing together again in friendship
G. Extreme wickedness or cruelty
H. Losing flesh; wasting away
I. Not definite or precise
J. Destroy; wipe out
K. Showing guilt
L. Deserving blame
M. Observable; understandable
N. Unbroken; uninjured
O. Future generations
P. Excited noise and activity
Q. Judging things on their practical consequences
R. Things made to be used up
S. Understood without being openly said
T. Mild or indirect expressions
U. Embarrassed
V. Relentlessly; unyielding
W. Openings; holes
X. Lying down flat
Y. About to happen

1984 VOCABULARY MAGIC SQUARES 1

A. PROLETARIAT
B. INCREDULOUS
C. RASH
D. BIGOTED
E. ORIFICES
F. IRRECONCILABLE
G. IMPENDING
H. SERVILE
I. EUPHEMISMS
J. INCRIMINATING
K. STRIDENT
L. EQUIVOCATION
M. CLANDESTINELY
N. ARBITRARY
O. INIMICAL
P. CAPITULATED

1. The lowest economic or social class
2. Without regard to a rule or law
3. Showing guilt
4. Openings; holes
5. About to happen
6. Not making a commitment on a matter
7. Gave up
8. Hasty and careless
9. Harmful; unfavorable
10. Unreasonably attached to an opinion or belief
11. Giving in because of fear
12. Having a harsh sound
13. Mild or indirect expressions
14. Not able to agree
15. Not believing
16. Done in a secret or underhanded manner

A=	B=	C=	D=
E=	F=	G=	H=
I=	J=	K=	L=
M=	N=	O=	P=

1984 VOCABULARY MATCHING SQUARES 1 KEY

A. PROLETARIAT
B. INCREDULOUS
C. RASH
D. BIGOTED
E. ORIFICES
F. IRRECONCILABLE
G. IMPENDING
H. SERVILE
I. EUPHEMISMS
J. INCRIMINATING
K. STRIDENT
L. EQUIVOCATION
M. CLANDESTINELY
N. ARBITRARY
O. INIMICAL
P. CAPITULATED

1. The lowest economic or social class
2. Without regard to a rule or law
3. Showing guilt
4. Openings; holes
5. About to happen
6. Not making a commitment on a matter
7. Gave up
8. Hasty and careless
9. Harmful; unfavorable
10. Unreasonably attached to an opinion or belief
11. Giving in because of fear
12. Having a harsh sound
13. Mild or indirect expressions
14. Not able to agree
15. Not believing
16. Done in a secret or underhanded manner

A=1	B=15	C=8	D=10
E=4	F=14	G=5	H=11
I=13	J=3	K=12	L=6
M=16	N=2	O=9	P=7

1984 VOCABULARY MATCHING SQUARES 2

A. DEGRADATION
B. INTEGRITY
C. SERVILE
D. ABYSS
E. SPURIOUS
F. VINDICATE
G. PURGES
H. STRIDENT
I. TORPID
J. METAPHYSICS
K. SINECURES
L. EXTRICATE
M. PRAGMATISM
N. RASH
O. AXIOM
P. COMMOTION

1. Statement taken to be true without proof
2. An attempt to explain reality and knowledge
3. Having a harsh sound
4. Worn or broken down condition
5. Lowest depth
6. False; not genuine
7. Very easy jobs that pay well
8. Hasty and careless
9. Excuse; absolve
10. Giving in because of fear
11. Judging things on their practical consequences
12. Set free; release
13. Dull; inactive
14. Excited noise and activity
15. Honesty; sincerity
16. Removal of undesirable people from a nation or party

A=	B=	C=	D=
E=	F=	G=	H=
I=	J=	K=	L=
M=	N=	O=	P=

1984 VOCABULARY MATCHING SQUARES 2 KEY

A. DEGRADATION
B. INTEGRITY
C. SERVILE
D. ABYSS
E. SPURIOUS
F. VINDICATE
G. PURGES
H. STRIDENT
I. TORPID
J. METAPHYSICS
K. SINECURES
L. EXTRICATE
M. PRAGMATISM
N. RASH
O. AXIOM
P. COMMOTION

1. Statement taken to be true without proof
2. An attempt to explain reality and knowledge
3. Having a harsh sound
4. Worn or broken down condition
5. Lowest depth
6. False; not genuine
7. Very easy jobs that pay well
8. Hasty and careless
9. Excuse; absolve
10. Giving in because of fear
11. Judging things on their practical consequences
12. Set free; release
13. Dull; inactive
14. Excited noise and activity
15. Honesty; sincerity
16. Removal of undesirable people from a nation or party

A=4	B=15	C=10	D=5
E=6	F=9	G=16	H=3
I=13	J=2	K=7	L=12
M=11	N=8	O=1	P=14

1984 VOCABULARY MATCHING SQUARES 3

A. LETHARGY
B. DIMINUTION
C. CALLOUSNESS
D. COMMOTION
E. FATUOUS
F. UNORTHODOXY
G. INCREDULITY
H. ABSURDITY
I. SERVILE
J. MALLEABLE
K. EMACIATION
L. INCRIMINATING
M. SINECURES
N. ORIFICES
O. IRRECONCILABLE
P. CAPITALISTS

1. Very easy jobs that pay well
2. Not holding generally accepted beliefs
3. Nonsense
4. Not able to agree
5. Showing guilt
6. An unfeeling manner; hard-heartedness
7. Drowsy dullness or lack of activity
8. Able to be shaped or molded
9. Losing flesh; wasting away
10. Excited noise and activity
11. Reduction; decrease
12. Giving in because of fear
13. Openings; holes
14. Silly; foolish
15. Lack of belief
16. People who use money to carry on business

A=	B=	C=	D=
E=	F=	G=	H=
I=	J=	K=	L=
M=	N=	O=	P=

1984 VOCABULARY MATCHING SQUARES 3 KEY

A. LETHARGY
B. DIMINUTION
C. CALLOUSNESS
D. COMMOTION
E. FATUOUS
F. UNORTHODOXY
G. INCREDULITY
H. ABSURDITY
I. SERVILE
J. MALLEABLE
K. EMACIATION
L. INCRIMINATING
M. SINECURES
N. ORIFICES
O. IRRECONCILABLE
P. CAPITALISTS

1. Very easy jobs that pay well
2. Not holding generally accepted beliefs
3. Nonsense
4. Not able to agree
5. Showing guilt
6. An unfeeling manner; hard-heartedness
7. Drowsy dullness or lack of activity
8. Able to be shaped or molded
9. Losing flesh; wasting away
10. Excited noise and activity
11. Reduction; decrease
12. Giving in because of fear
13. Openings; holes
14. Silly; foolish
15. Lack of belief
16. People who use money to carry on business

A=7	B=11	C=6	D=10
E=14	F=2	G=15	H=3
I=12	J=8	K=9	L=5
M=1	N=13	O=4	P=16

1984 VOCABULARY MATCHING SQUARES 4

A. BIGOTED
B. OLIGARCHIES
C. TORPID
D. INDIGNATION
E. INTEGRITY
F. IMPREGNABLE
G. INIQUITY
H. LUMINOUS
I. ABASHED
J. ENVELOPING
K. TACITLY
L. ACCUMULATED
M. ABYSS
N. ATROCITY
O. SUCCUMBED
P. MALLEABLE

1. Lowest depth
2. Won't give in to force or persuasion
3. Shining by its own light
4. Gave way; yielded
5. Collected
6. Dull; inactive
7. Unreasonably attached to an opinion or belief
8. Surrounding
9. Understood without being openly said
10. Anger combined with disapproval
11. Governments ruled by only a few people
12. Embarrassed
13. Extreme wickedness or cruelty
14. Honesty; sincerity
15. Wickedness
16. Able to be shaped or molded

A=	B=	C=	D=
E=	F=	G=	H=
I=	J=	K=	L=
M=	N=	O=	P=

1984 VOCABULARY MATCHING SQUARES 4 KEY

A. BIGOTED
B. OLIGARCHIES
C. TORPID
D. INDIGNATION
E. INTEGRITY
F. IMPREGNABLE
G. INIQUITY
H. LUMINOUS
I. ABASHED
J. ENVELOPING
K. TACITLY
L. ACCUMULATED
M. ABYSS
N. ATROCITY
O. SUCCUMBED
P. MALLEABLE

1. Lowest depth
2. Won't give in to force or persuasion
3. Shining by its own light
4. Gave way; yielded
5. Collected
6. Dull; inactive
7. Unreasonably attached to an opinion or belief
8. Surrounding
9. Understood without being openly said
10. Anger combined with disapproval
11. Governments ruled by only a few people
12. Embarrassed
13. Extreme wickedness or cruelty
14. Honesty; sincerity
15. Wickedness
16. Able to be shaped or molded

A=7	B=11	C=6	D=10
E=14	F=2	G=15	H=3
I=12	J=8	K=9	L=5
M=1	N=13	O=4	P=16

1984 VOCABULARY WORD SEARCH 1

```
S U C C U M B E D V A B S U R D I T Y N
C J G J X S T D O R I F I C E S S Z O M
A G N I P O L E V N E N R H R O P I N T
L V C C S M U G L Y N P D A C M T Q O R
L V D T P F Y R R C J T U I S A T Y I W
O T H S S Y B A O L I G A R C H I E S R
U Z W K Z J I D R H F L K O G A D I I G
S W I M S D B A K B I N V J Y E T N C C
N I D N I T W T B S I I Q G T C S E E S
E N M S T T F I M A U T A X I O M X R F
S U B P N I G O N Q S N R N C M S O P M
S U P P E O M N E V B H J A O M I R V F
S I R H T N S I S P I D E F R J M A A S
A N O E O K D E D T M O F D T Y E B G W
B I D G P N J I R A R Z L A A F H L U K
O Q I Y I R Y K N V T I C A V C P Y E K
T U G G N D G P L G I I D C T R U N P B
A I I N M D I P R O T L N E H E E Z F H
G T E B O M Z E A L O T E G N O G R A J
E Y S R P P T C Y X Y G R A H T E L H N
```

About to happen (9)
Accuracy; exactness (9)
An unfeeling manner; hard-heartedness (11)
Combination of pleasant sounds (7)
Damage or destruction done as an attack (8)
Drowsy dullness or lack of activity (8)
Dull; inactive (6)
Embarrassed (7)
Excuse; absolve (9)
Extreme wickedness or cruelty (8)
Frightening (12)
Gave way; yielded (9)
Giving in because of fear (7)
Government production and distribution of goods (9)
Governments ruled by only a few people (11)
Hasty and careless (4)
Having a harsh sound (8)
Having great power or influence (10)
In a way that is too pleased with oneself (6)
Language of a special group (6)
Lowest depth (5)
Marvelous examples (9)

Mild or indirect expressions (10)
Nonsense (9)
Not definite or precise (5)
Not making a commitment on a matter (12)
Openings; holes (8)
Person who shows too much enthusiasm; a fanatic (6)
Relentlessly; unyielding (10)
Removal of undesirable people from a nation or party (6)
Secondary (10)
Statement taken to be true without proof (5)
Surrounding (10)
Unbroken; uninjured (9)
Understood without being openly said (7)
Unreasonably attached to an opinion or belief (7)
Wickedness (8)
Without regard to a rule or law (9)
Worn or broken down condition (11)

1984 VOCABULARY WORD SEARCH 1 KEY

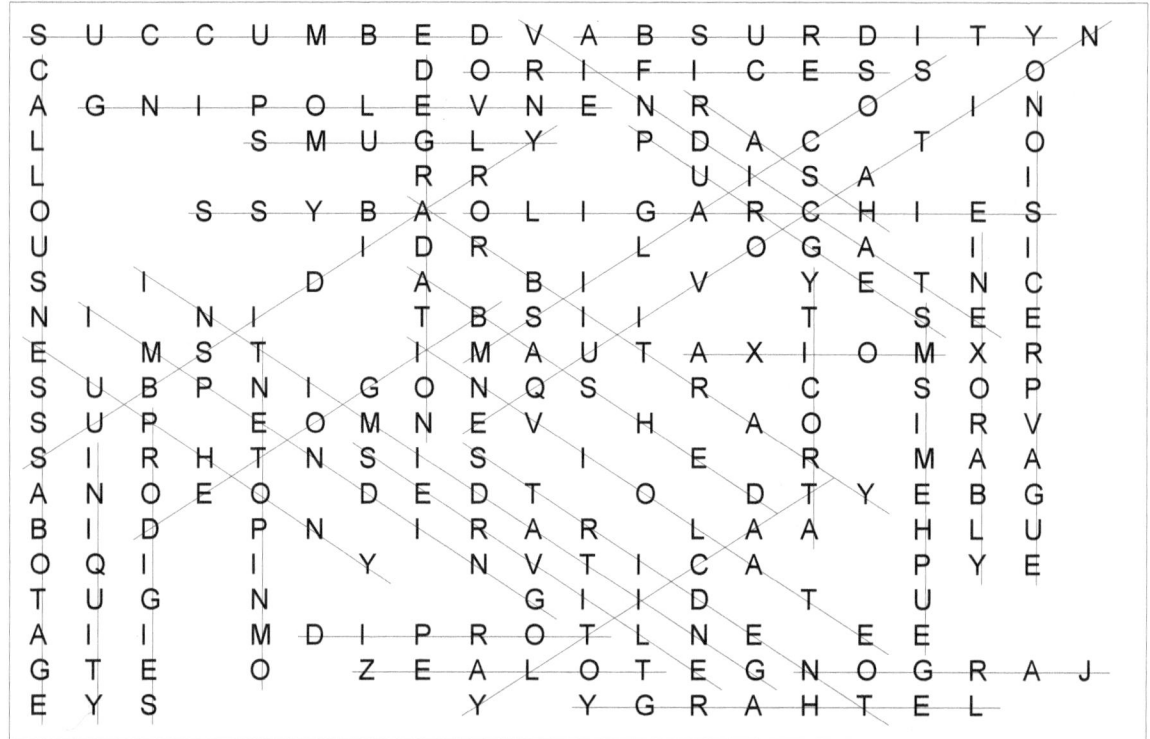

About to happen (9)
Accuracy; exactness (9)
An unfeeling manner; hard-heartedness (11)
Combination of pleasant sounds (7)
Damage or destruction done as an attack (8)
Drowsy dullness or lack of activity (8)
Dull; inactive (6)
Embarrassed (7)
Excuse; absolve (9)
Extreme wickedness or cruelty (8)
Frightening (12)
Gave way; yielded (9)
Giving in because of fear (7)
Government production and distribution of goods (9)
Governments ruled by only a few people (11)
Hasty and careless (4)
Having a harsh sound (8)
Having great power or influence (10)
In a way that is too pleased with oneself (6)
Language of a special group (6)
Lowest depth (5)
Marvelous examples (9)

Mild or indirect expressions (10)
Nonsense (9)
Not definite or precise (5)
Not making a commitment on a matter (12)
Openings; holes (8)
Person who shows too much enthusiasm; a fanatic (6)
Relentlessly; unyielding (10)
Removal of undesirable people from a nation or party (6)
Secondary (10)
Statement taken to be true without proof (5)
Surrounding (10)
Unbroken; uninjured (9)
Understood without being openly said (7)
Unreasonably attached to an opinion or belief (7)
Wickedness (8)
Without regard to a rule or law (9)
Worn or broken down condition (11)

1984 VOCABULARY WORD SEARCH 2

```
A R B I T R A R Y I D E O L O G I C A L
U T W F S D Z S U O U T A F J M C Z S W
N A B M U E E R A D I C A T E A H N C P
O C I E C Z A G K B T I N T E G R I T Y
R I G X C I L R E N O I T A D A R G E D
T T O T U N O E D M S T R I D E N T O W
H L T R M I T S Q Z P S A O K D S V C N
O Y E I B T M P H U C I P G N G B M O V
D C D C E U U R X A I O R R E I P J N C
O E Y A D R H W E B R V N I Q A C P V Y
X E M T G C S T M Y K Q O T C J T A O E
Y T D E H S A B A S E I H C R A G I L O
M A S W A L R X V S K G U I A I L I U J
R C X W O N P X I F B M N T S T V Q T S
K I P I S Z O Z L O U I Z V O R I E E C
T D V S M N L R D L M C B Q E R C O D P
I N I Q U I T Y A I Q J J S N D P B N R
I I V A G U E T C L U M I N O U S I N S
W V M A L L E A B L E L B A P L A P D B
K C X X Y D L O R I F I C E S S Z Z G L
```

Able to be shaped or molded (9)
Based on experiment and observation (9)
Behavior; manner (8)
Collected (11)
Damage or destruction done as an attack (8)
Destroy; wipe out (9)
Dull; inactive (6)
Easily seen or heard and recognized (8)
Embarrassed (7)
Examined carefully (11)
Excuse; absolve (9)
Expressing one thing and meaning another (8)
Gave way; yielded (9)
Giving in because of fear (7)
Governments ruled by only a few people (11)
Harmful; unfavorable (8)
Hasty and careless (4)
Having a harsh sound (8)
Having folds or winding curves (10)
Having to do with the opinions of a person or political movement (11)
Honesty; sincerity (9)

In a way that is too pleased with oneself (6)
Language of a special group (6)
Lowest depth (5)
Not definite or precise (5)
Not holding generally accepted beliefs (11)
Not making a commitment on a matter (12)
Openings; holes (8)
Person who shows too much enthusiasm; a fanatic (6)
Planned; designed (9)
Removal of undesirable people from a nation or party (6)
Set free; release (9)
Shining by its own light (8)
Silly; foolish (7)
Statement taken to be true without proof (5)
Unbroken; uninjured (9)
Understood without being openly said (7)
Unreasonably attached to an opinion or belief (7)
Wickedness (8)
Without regard to a rule or law (9)
Worn or broken down condition (11)

1984 VOCABULARY WORD SEARCH 2 KEY

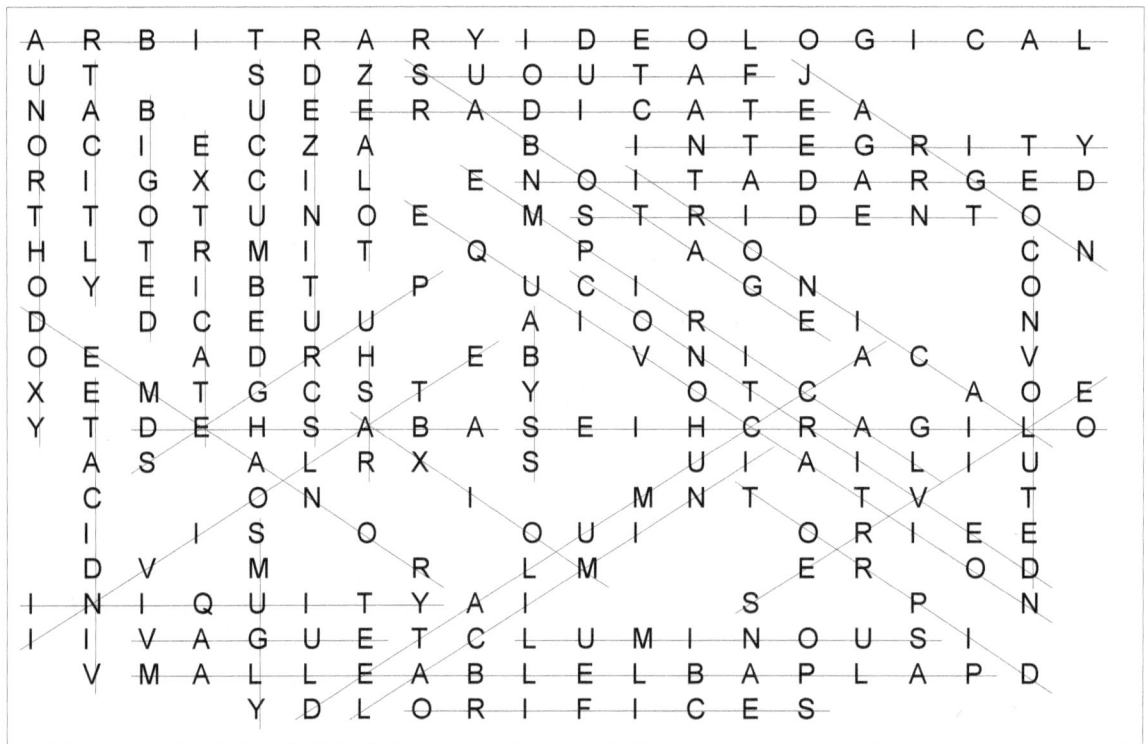

Able to be shaped or molded (9)
Based on experiment and observation (9)
Behavior; manner (8)
Collected (11)
Damage or destruction done as an attack (8)
Destroy; wipe out (9)
Dull; inactive (6)
Easily seen or heard and recognized (8)
Embarrassed (7)
Examined carefully (11)
Excuse; absolve (9)
Expressing one thing and meaning another (8)
Gave way; yielded (9)
Giving in because of fear (7)
Governments ruled by only a few people (11)
Harmful; unfavorable (8)
Hasty and careless (4)
Having a harsh sound (8)
Having folds or winding curves (10)
Having to do with the opinions of a person or political movement (11)
Honesty; sincerity (9)

In a way that is too pleased with oneself (6)
Language of a special group (6)
Lowest depth (5)
Not definite or precise (5)
Not holding generally accepted beliefs (11)
Not making a commitment on a matter (12)
Openings; holes (8)
Person who shows too much enthusiasm; a fanatic (6)
Planned; designed (9)
Removal of undesirable people from a nation or party (6)
Set free; release (9)
Shining by its own light (8)
Silly; foolish (7)
Statement taken to be true without proof (5)
Unbroken; uninjured (9)
Understood without being openly said (7)
Unreasonably attached to an opinion or belief (7)
Wickedness (8)
Without regard to a rule or law (9)
Worn or broken down condition (11)

1984 VOCABULARY WORD SEARCH 3

```
E X T R I C A T E I D E H S A B A E E G
P S E P M T D F L N H L F G V Q G L Z Z
M G T O P O E Y A C H B D P G Q I B E V
S L A S E R T R C R O A L P Z V X A I Z
I Y C T N P A S I E X N X P R N L L R P
T N I E D I L D M D J G V E B O L I O B
A O D R I D U T I U O E S O T J S C N G
M H A I N D T H N L F R Y V L E G N I R
G P R T G Z I A I I Z P L G G U S O C L
A U E Y B N P G B T X M G R S N T C A X
R E L E T H A R G Y T I U Q I N I E L S
P C B P T R C T L G S P M B O O U R D H
P T Y H C X P T I K M S S I Q G F R S Z
N B T H B Y I A L O U F T X A R A I T F
O R I F I C E S L O N O S V N A T V R Z
Y E C G A A M F N P M N P R K J U P I Q
S V O T O J X I E M A C I A T I O N D F
R C R D N T M I O W G B S S C P U P E Q
D T T B R U E C O R V M L H L C S G N Q
K Q A K L N J D S M S I M E H P U E T J
```

ABASHED	EUPHEMISMS	IRONICAL	PURGES
ABYSS	EUPHONY	IRRECONCILABLE	RASH
ATROCITY	EXTRICATE	JARGON	SERVILE
AXIOM	FATUOUS	LETHARGY	SMUGLY
BIGOTED	IMPENDING	LUMINOUS	STRIDENT
CAPITULATED	IMPREGNABLE	OLIGARCHIES	TACITLY
COMMOTION	INCREDULITY	ORIFICES	TORPID
CONVOLUTED	INDIGNATION	PALPABLE	VAGUE
EMACIATION	INIMICAL	POSTERITY	ZEALOT
ERADICATE	INIQUITY	PRAGMATISM	

1984 VOCABULARY WORD SEARCH 3 KEY

ABASHED	EUPHEMISMS	IRONICAL	PURGES
ABYSS	EUPHONY	IRRECONCILABLE	RASH
ATROCITY	EXTRICATE	JARGON	SERVILE
AXIOM	FATUOUS	LETHARGY	SMUGLY
BIGOTED	IMPENDING	LUMINOUS	STRIDENT
CAPITULATED	IMPREGNABLE	OLIGARCHIES	TACITLY
COMMOTION	INCREDULITY	ORIFICES	TORPID
CONVOLUTED	INDIGNATION	PALPABLE	VAGUE
EMACIATION	INIMICAL	POSTERITY	ZEALOT
ERADICATE	INIQUITY	PRAGMATISM	

1984 VOCABULARY WORD SEARCH 4

```
M A L L E A B L E A T R O C I T Y E R H
S N O I T A C I F I M A R S Y S L O C P
S U B S I D I A R Y X N S L X I N E H L
H M A B A S H E D I O Y T H V A T S T P
T E D S T S O H O I B I G R E A E O Y T
G T E H G E B M T A C N E M L Q L T E T
P A V B G G B P N A O S E O U A L M E R
F P I G H R M G T I X D I I E H A I U S
W H R G B U X I T Y P V V Z V C C N P J
S Y T G S P B U N W N O R T I F I F H J
E S N N X C N S E I C I T A O Y R A O P
R I O X M I M M X A M N T E S R I L N X
A C C U M U L A T E D I B V N H P L Y W
D S U I G Z L I R R O Q C I A T M I V V
I D D L D Y O W I N N U N A G G E B D C
C L Y P P N S E C I F I R O L O U L R L
A N O G R A J T A F A T U O U S T E L Z
T H V G N K B J T S C Y S T R I D E N T
E P A L P A B L E P R O D I G I E S D B
S P U R I O U S E V I N D I C A T E Z Z
```

ABASHED	EMACIATION	JARGON	SMUGLY
ABYSS	EMPIRICAL	MALLEABLE	SPURIOUS
ACCUMULATED	EQUIVOCATION	METAPHYSICS	STRIDENT
ATROCITY	ERADICATE	OMNIPOTENT	SUBSIDIARY
AXIOM	EUPHONY	ORIFICES	TACITLY
BIGOTED	EXTRICATE	PALPABLE	TORPID
CONSUMPTION	FATUOUS	PRODIGIES	VAGUE
CONTRIVED	INFALLIBLE	PURGES	VINDICATE
CULPABLE	INIMICAL	RAMIFICATIONS	ZEALOT
DEMEANOR	INIQUITY	RASH	
DIMINUTION	INVIOLATE	SERVILE	

1984 VOCABULARY WORD SEARCH 4 KEY

```
M A L L E A B L E A T R O C I T Y E R
S N O I T A C I F I M A R S Y   L O
S U B S I D I A R Y X N S L   I N E
    M A B A S H E D I O Y T   V A T     T
    E D     S O     O I B I   R E A E O
    T E     E     M T A C N E M L Q L   E
    A V     G   P N A O S E O U A L M E
    P I     R M T I   D I I E   A I N E U
    H R     U   I T   P V V Z   C C N F P
    Y T   S P   U N   N O R T I   I F H
E   S N   N     N S E I C T A O   R A O
R   I O     I M   X A M N T E S R I L N
A   C C U M U L A T E D I B V N H P L Y
D   S U I G       I R   O Q C I A T M I
I     D L     O   I N   U   A G G E B D
C       Y   P N S E C I F I R O L O U L
A   N O G R A J   A F A T U O U S T E
T           B     T       Y S T R I D E N T
E P A L P A B L E P R O D I G I E S   D
S P U R I O U S E V I N D I C A T E
```

ABASHED	EMACIATION	JARGON	SMUGLY
ABYSS	EMPIRICAL	MALLEABLE	SPURIOUS
ACCUMULATED	EQUIVOCATION	METAPHYSICS	STRIDENT
ATROCITY	ERADICATE	OMNIPOTENT	SUBSIDIARY
AXIOM	EUPHONY	ORIFICES	TACITLY
BIGOTED	EXTRICATE	PALPABLE	TORPID
CONSUMPTION	FATUOUS	PRODIGIES	VAGUE
CONTRIVED	INFALLIBLE	PURGES	VINDICATE
CULPABLE	INIMICAL	RAMIFICATIONS	ZEALOT
DEMEANOR	INIQUITY	RASH	
DIMINUTION	INVIOLATE	SERVILE	

1984 VOCABULARY CROSSWORD 1

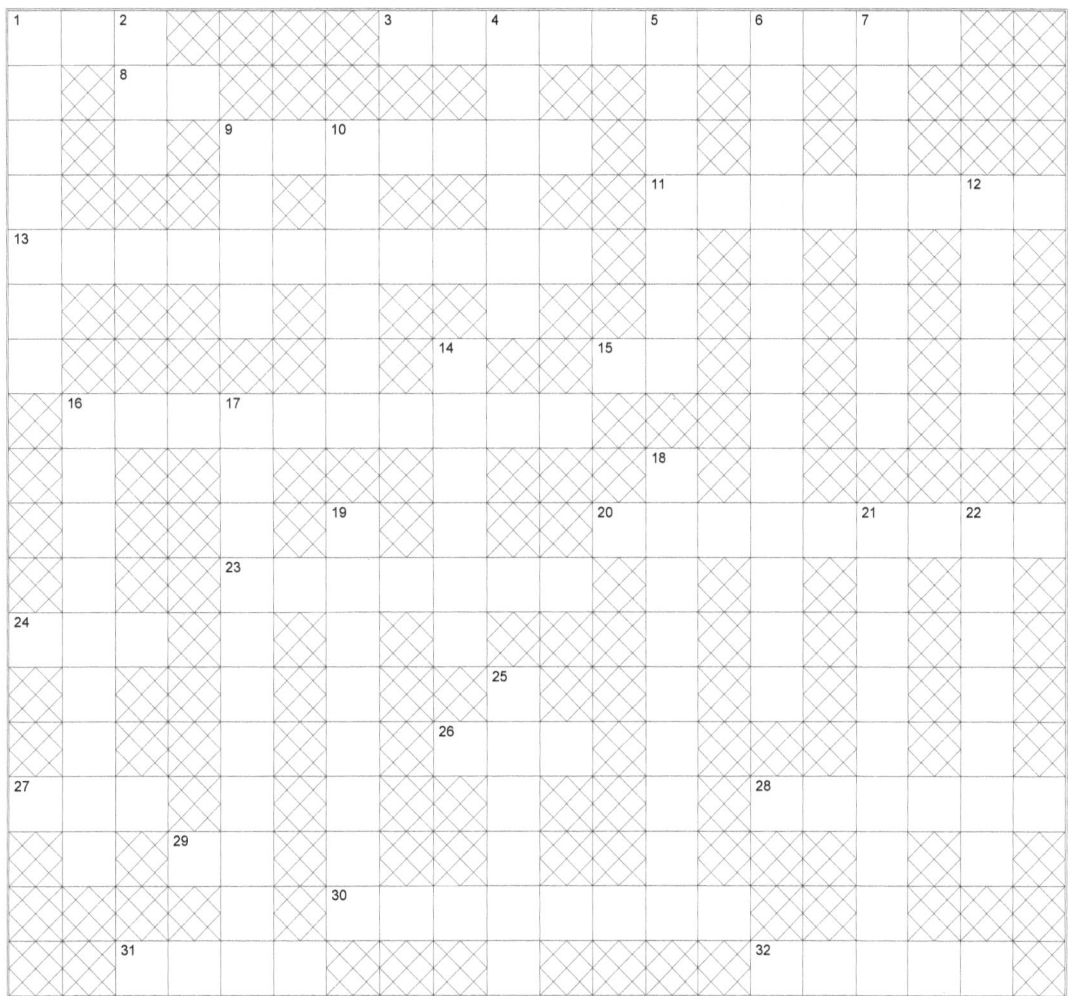

Across
1. It provides warmth and light to the earth
3. Jumping from one topic to another
8. Either's partner
9. Silly; foolish
11. Harmful; unfavorable
13. Too much to be endured
15. Belonging to me
16. Secondary
20. Based on experiment and observation
23. Combination of pleasant sounds
24. Belonging to us
26. A positive answer
27. Allow
28. Removal of undesirable people from a nation or party
29. A negative answer
30. Damage or destruction done as an attack
31. Hasty and careless
32. Lowest depth

Down
1. Giving in because of fear
2. Neither's partner
4. In a way that is too pleased with oneself
5. Understood without being openly said
6. Branches; subdivisions
7. Shining by its own light
9. Season between summer and winter
10. Dull; inactive
12. Statement taken to be true without proof
14. Language of a special group
16. Gave way; yielded
17. Unnecessary
18. About to happen
19. False; not genuine
21. Honesty; sincerity
22. Embarrassed
25. Person who shows too much enthusiasm; a fanatic

1984 VOCABULARY CROSSWORD 1 KEY

Across
1. It provides warmth and light to the earth
3. Jumping from one topic to another
8. Either's partner
9. Silly; foolish
11. Harmful; unfavorable
13. Too much to be endured
15. Belonging to me
16. Secondary
20. Based on experiment and observation
23. Combination of pleasant sounds
24. Belonging to us
26. A positive answer
27. Allow
28. Removal of undesirable people from a nation or party
29. A negative answer
30. Damage or destruction done as an attack
31. Hasty and careless
32. Lowest depth

Down
1. Giving in because of fear
2. Neither's partner
4. In a way that is too pleased with oneself
5. Understood without being openly said
6. Branches; subdivisions
7. Shining by its own light
9. Season between summer and winter
10. Dull; inactive
12. Statement taken to be true without proof
14. Language of a special group
16. Gave way; yielded
17. Unnecessary
18. About to happen
19. False; not genuine
21. Honesty; sincerity
22. Embarrassed
25. Person who shows too much enthusiasm; a fanatic

1984 VOCABULARY CROSSWORD 2

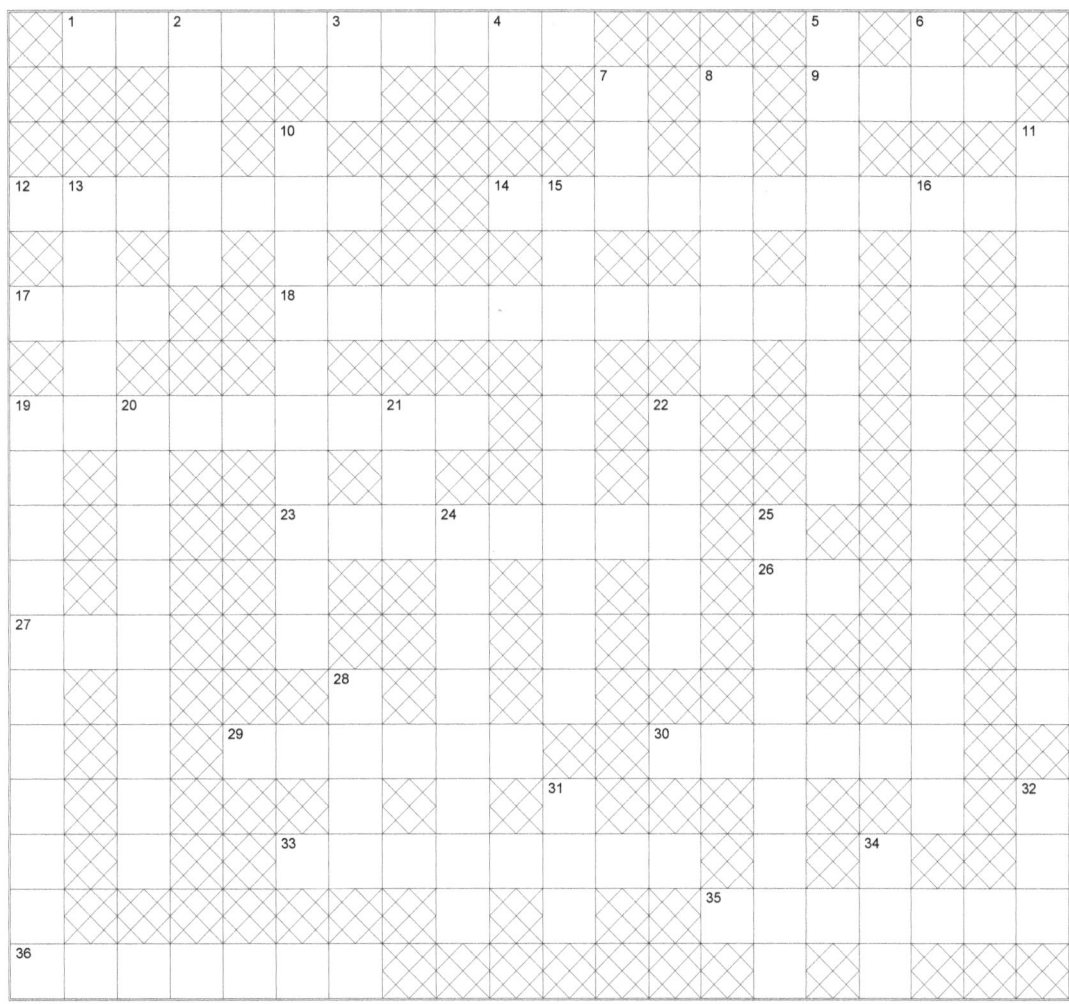

Across
1. Surrounding
9. Hasty and careless
12. Silly; foolish
14. Arranging things one above the other by rank
17. Belonging to him
18. Unnecessary
19. About to happen
23. Extreme wickedness or cruelty
26. Belonging to me
27. A falsehood; an untruth
29. Dull; inactive
30. Language of a special group
33. Behavior; manner
35. Understood without being openly said
36. Combination of pleasant sounds

Down
2. Not definite or precise
3. Either's partner
4. A negative answer
5. Accuracy; exactness
6. Ourselves
7. First number
8. Person who shows too much enthusiasm; a fanatic
10. Secondary
11. Governments ruled by only a few people
13. Statement taken to be true without proof
15. Free from error
16. Frightening
19. Too much to be endured
20. Future generations
21. Neither's partner
22. Lowest depth
24. Openings; holes
25. Based on experiment and observation
28. A fact; accurate
31. A coordinating conjunction
32. A feeling of happiness
34. Opposite of small

1984 VOCABULARY CROSSWORD 2 KEY

Across
1. Surrounding
9. Hasty and careless
12. Silly; foolish
14. Arranging things one above the other by rank
17. Belonging to him
18. Unnecessary
19. About to happen
23. Extreme wickedness or cruelty
26. Belonging to me
27. A falsehood; an untruth
29. Dull; inactive
30. Language of a special group
33. Behavior; manner
35. Understood without being openly said
36. Combination of pleasant sounds

Down
2. Not definite or precise
3. Either's partner
4. A negative answer
5. Accuracy; exactness
6. Ourselves
7. First number
8. Person who shows too much enthusiasm; a fanatic
10. Secondary
11. Governments ruled by only a few people
13. Statement taken to be true without proof
15. Free from error
16. Frightening
19. Too much to be endured
20. Future generations
21. Neither's partner
22. Lowest depth
24. Openings; holes
25. Based on experiment and observation
28. A fact; accurate
31. A coordinating conjunction
32. A feeling of happiness
34. Opposite of small

1984 VOCABULARY CROSSWORD 3

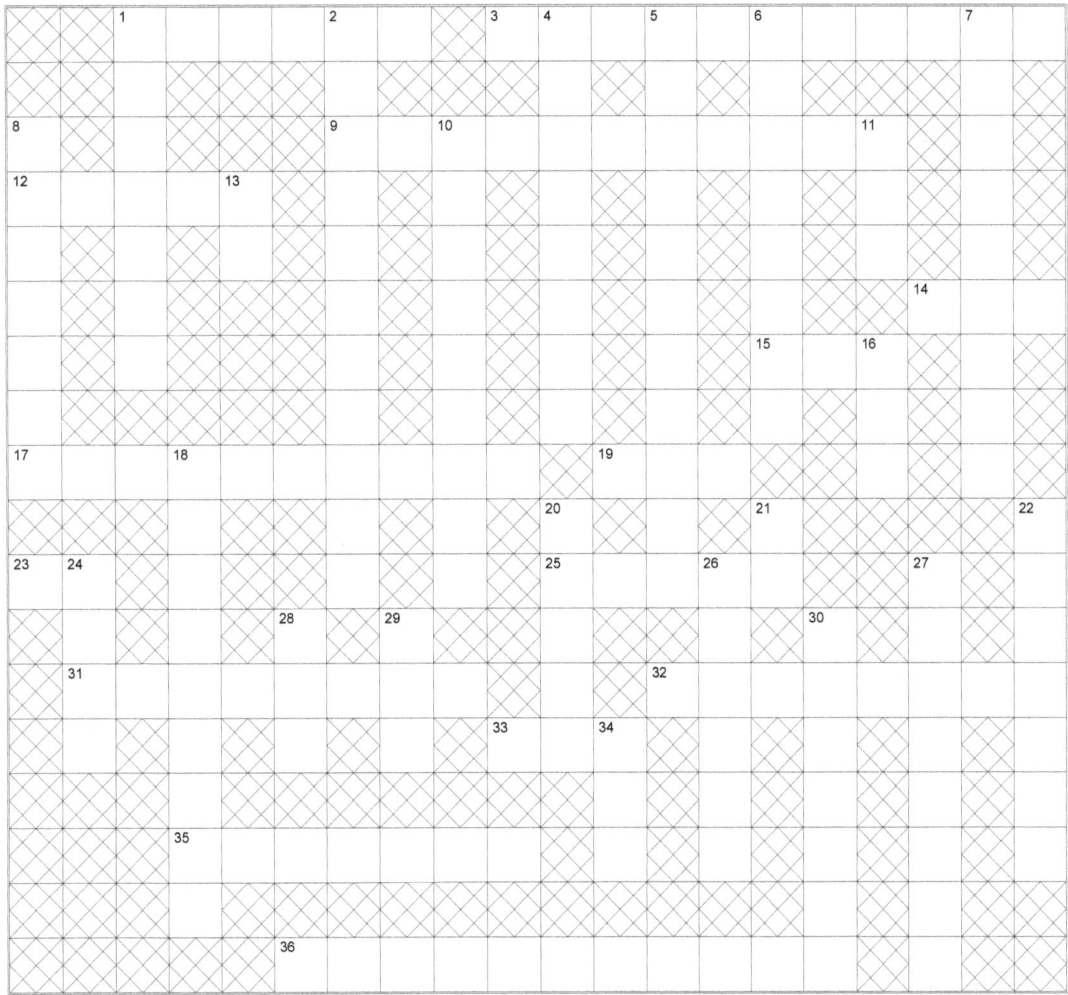

Across
1. Dull; inactive
3. Examined carefully
9. Jumping from one topic to another
12. Statement taken to be true without proof
14. Belonging to him
15. A coordinating conjunction
17. Secondary
19. Also
23. Either's partner
25. Lowest depth
31. False; not genuine
32. Shining by its own light
33. Allow
35. Combination of pleasant sounds
36. Gave up

Down
1. Understood without being openly said
2. Anger combined with disapproval
4. Deserving blame
5. Not holding generally accepted beliefs
6. Harmful; unfavorable
7. Based on experiment and observation
8. Silly; foolish
10. Very easy jobs that pay well
11. A positive answer
13. Belonging to me
16. Man's best friend
18. Gave way; yielded
20. Not definite or precise
21. Ourselves
22. Embarrassed
24. Hasty and careless
26. In a way that is too pleased with oneself
27. Expressing one thing and meaning another
28. A falsehood; an untruth
29. Belonging to us
30. Unreasonably attached to an opinion or belief
34. More than 1 & less than 3

1984 VOCABULARY CROSSWORD 3 KEY

```
         1T  O  R  P  I  2D       3S  4C  R  5U  T  6I  N  I  7Z  E  D
             A           N            U      N         M
 8F     C            9D  E  10S  L  T  O  R  I  11L  Y     P
 12A  X  I  O  13M   I      I      P      R  M      E     I
     T     T     Y      G      N     A      T     I     S     R
     U     L           N      E     B     H     C      14H  I  S
     O     Y           A      C     L     O   15A  N  16D  C
     U                T      U     E     D     L         O     A
 17S  U  B  18S  I  D  I  A  R  Y      19T  O  O         G     L
             U            O       E   20V     X   21U              22A
 23O 24R     C            N       S   25A  B  Y  26S  S      27I     B
        A          28L       29O         G          M        30B     R  A
     31S  P  U  R  I  O  U  S         32L  U  M  I  N  O  U  S
        H     M        E        R   33L  34E  T   G     G     N  H
              B                         W     L      O      I     E
          35E  U  P  H  O  N  Y         O     Y      T      C  D
              D                                      E      A
                  36C  A  P  I  T  U  L  A  T  E  D        L
```

Across
1. Dull; inactive
3. Examined carefully
9. Jumping from one topic to another
12. Statement taken to be true without proof
14. Belonging to him
15. A coordinating conjunction
17. Secondary
19. Also
23. Either's partner
25. Lowest depth
31. False; not genuine
32. Shining by its own light
33. Allow
35. Combination of pleasant sounds
36. Gave up

Down
1. Understood without being openly said
2. Anger combined with disapproval
4. Deserving blame
5. Not holding generally accepted beliefs
6. Harmful; unfavorable
7. Based on experiment and observation
8. Silly; foolish
10. Very easy jobs that pay well
11. A positive answer
13. Belonging to me
16. Man's best friend
18. Gave way; yielded
20. Not definite or precise
21. Ourselves
22. Embarrassed
24. Hasty and careless
26. In a way that is too pleased with oneself
27. Expressing one thing and meaning another
28. A falsehood; an untruth
29. Belonging to us
30. Unreasonably attached to an opinion or belief
34. More than 1 & less than 3

1984 VOCABULARY CROSSWORD 4

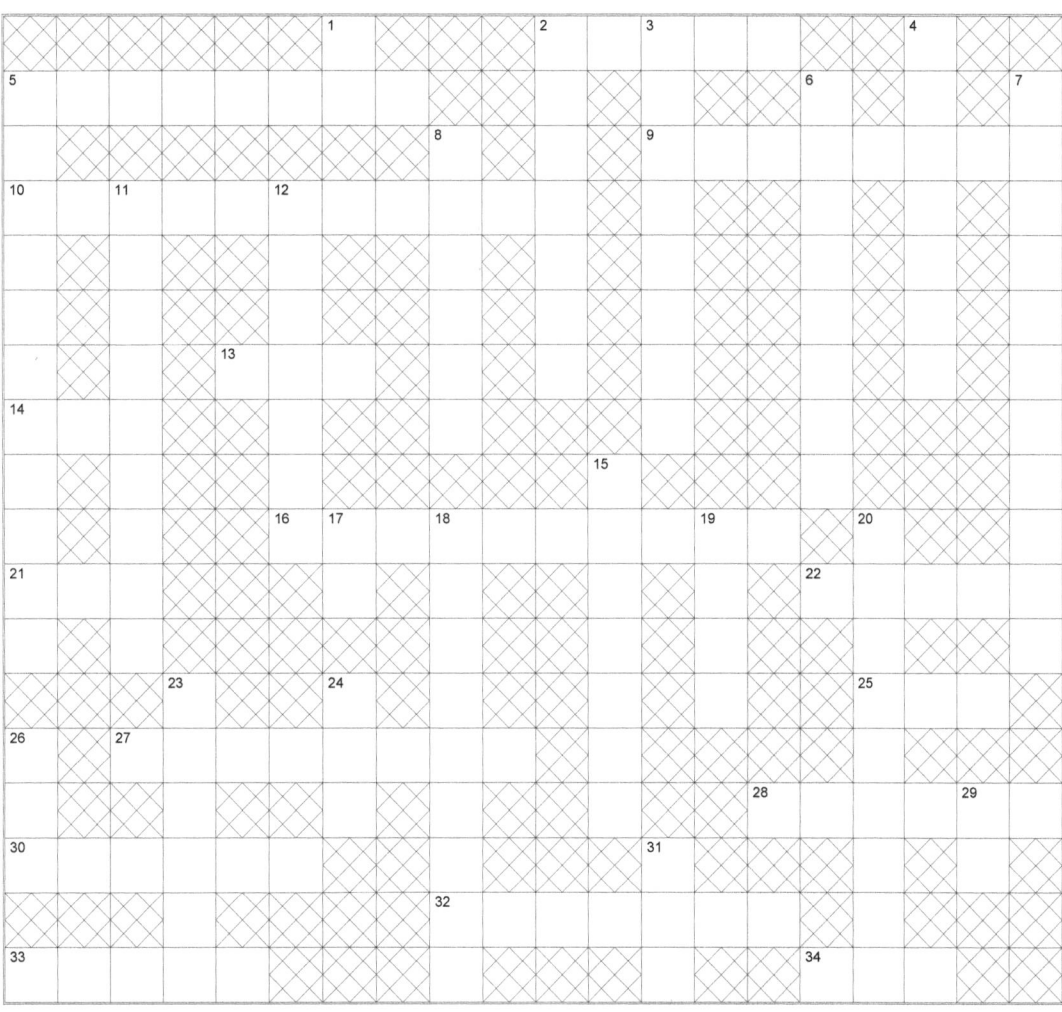

Across
2. Statement taken to be true without proof
5. Behavior; manner
9. Expressing one thing and meaning another
10. Unnecessary
13. Belonging to us
14. First number
16. Secondary
21. Allow
22. Not definite or precise
25. A falsehood; an untruth
27. Shining by its own light
28. Person who shows too much enthusiasm; a fanatic
30. In a way that is too pleased with oneself
32. Combination of pleasant sounds
33. Lowest depth
34. A positive answer

Down
1. A negative answer
2. Embarrassed
3. Harmful; unfavorable
4. Understood without being openly said
5. Jumping from one topic to another
6. Wickedness
7. Governments ruled by only a few people
8. Dull; inactive
11. Future generations
12. Silly; foolish
15. Unreasonably attached to an opinion or belief
17. Ourselves
18. Gave way; yielded
19. Hasty and careless
20. Able to be shaped or molded
23. Removal of undesirable people from a nation or party
24. A coordinating conjunction
26. Belonging to him
29. Either's partner
31. Also

1984 VOCABULARY CROSSWORD 4 KEY

			¹N				²A	³X	I	O	M		⁴T		
⁵D	E	M	E	A	N	O	R		N			⁶I	A		⁷O
E						⁸T	A		⁹I	R	O	N	I	C	A	L
¹⁰S	U	¹¹P	E	¹²F	L	U	O	U	S		M		I		I		I
U		O		A		R		P		E		I		Q		T		G
L		S		T			P		E		C		U		L		A
T		T		¹³O	U	R		I		D		A		I		Y		R
¹⁴O	N	E			O		D				L			T			C
R		R			U				¹⁵B					Y			H
I		I		¹⁶S	¹⁷U	¹⁸B	S	I	D	I	A	¹⁹R	Y		²⁰M			I
²¹L	E	T			S		U			G		A		²²V	A	G	U	E
Y		Y					C			O		S		L				S
			²³P		²⁴A	C			T		H		²⁵L	I	E
²⁶H	²⁷L	U	M	I	N	O	U	S		E				L	
I		R			D		M			D		²⁸Z	E	A	L	²⁹O	T
³⁰S	M	U	G	L	Y		B		³¹T				B		R
		E				³²E	U	P	H	O	N	Y		L	
³³A	B	Y	S	S			D			O			³⁴Y	E	S

Across
2. Statement taken to be true without proof
5. Behavior; manner
9. Expressing one thing and meaning another
10. Unnecessary
13. Belonging to us
14. First number
16. Secondary
21. Allow
22. Not definite or precise
25. A falsehood; an untruth
27. Shining by its own light
28. Person who shows too much enthusiasm; a fanatic
30. In a way that is too pleased with oneself
32. Combination of pleasant sounds
33. Lowest depth
34. A positive answer

Down
1. A negative answer
2. Embarrassed
3. Harmful; unfavorable
4. Understood without being openly said
5. Jumping from one topic to another
6. Wickedness
7. Governments ruled by only a few people
8. Dull; inactive
11. Future generations
12. Silly; foolish
15. Unreasonably attached to an opinion or belief
17. Ourselves
18. Gave way; yielded
19. Hasty and careless
20. Able to be shaped or molded
23. Removal of undesirable people from a nation or party
24. A coordinating conjunction
26. Belonging to him
29. Either's partner
31. Also

1984 VOCABULARY JUGGLE LETTERS 1

1. IRLEESV = 1. _____
   Giving in because of fear

2. HRLTYAEG = 2. _____
   Drowsy dullness or lack of activity

3. ONCNILOACIRIET = 3. _____
   Bringing together again in friendship

4. TGITINNAIMDI = 4. _____
   Frightening

5. NRCISOEPI = 5. _____
   Accuracy; exactness

6. OSMUPNOCTIN = 6. _____
   Things made to be used up

7. SASYB = 7. _____
   Lowest depth

8. UNESAOLSSCL = 8. _____
   An unfeeling manner; hard-heartedness

9. LCUBEPLA = 9. _____
   Deserving blame

10. UNDOMNIITI =10. _____
    Reduction; decrease

11. IGONTANDNII =11. _____
    Anger combined with disapproval

12. LALIBENETRO =12. _____
    Too much to be endured

13. TUAUSFO =13. _____
    Silly; foolish

14. EPGRSU =14. _____
    Removal of undesirable people from a nation or party

15. OONIOMTMC =15. _____
    Excited noise and activity

Copyrighted Materials

1984 VOCABULARY JUGGLE LETTERS 1 KEY

1. IRLEESV = 1. SERVILE
   Giving in because of fear

2. HRLTYAEG = 2. LETHARGY
   Drowsy dullness or lack of activity

3. ONCNILOACIRIET = 3. RECONCILIATION
   Bringing together again in friendship

4. TGITINNAIMDI = 4. INTIMIDATING
   Frightening

5. NRCISOEPI = 5. PRECISION
   Accuracy; exactness

6. OSMUPNOCTIN = 6. CONSUMPTION
   Things made to be used up

7. SASYB = 7. ABYSS
   Lowest depth

8. UNESAOLSSCL = 8. CALLOUSNESS
   An unfeeling manner; hard-heartedness

9. LCUBEPLA = 9. CULPABLE
   Deserving blame

10. UNDOMNIITI = 10. DIMINUTION
    Reduction; decrease

11. IGONTANDNII = 11. INDIGNATION
    Anger combined with disapproval

12. LALIBENETRO = 12. INTOLERABLE
    Too much to be endured

13. TUAUSFO = 13. FATUOUS
    Silly; foolish

14. EPGRSU = 14. PURGES
    Removal of undesirable people from a nation or party

15. OONIOMTMC = 15. COMMOTION
    Excited noise and activity

1984 VOCABULARY JUGGLE LETTERS 2

1. IANDITTIGIMN = 1. _____
   Frightening

2. MTNCOOMIO = 2. _____
   Excited noise and activity

3. YTPIRETSO = 3. _____
   Future generations

4. LOLEGAICODI = 4. _____
   Having to do with the opinions of a person or political movement

5. DMEIIGNNP = 5. _____
   About to happen

6. DCEZUTISNRI = 6. _____
   Examined carefully

7. LIOCIAGSHER = 7. _____
   Governments ruled by only a few people

8. OTESAAGB = 8. _____
   Damage or destruction done as an attack

9. YRIETNGTI = 9. _____
   Honesty; sincerity

10. COINSERPI =10. _____
    Accuracy; exactness

11. SORICEIF =11. _____
    Openings; holes

12. ATPAMISRGM =12. _____
    Judging things on their practical consequences

13. VUDETOCONL =13. _____
    Having folds or winding curves

14. XBYEANRLIO =14. _____
    Relentlessly; unyielding

15. ACUELBPL =15. _____
    Deserving blame

Copyrighted Materials

1984 VOCABULARY JUGGLE LETTERS 2 KEY

1. IANDITTIGIMN = 1. INTIMIDATING
   Frightening

2. MTNCOOMIO = 2. COMMOTION
   Excited noise and activity

3. YTPIRETSO = 3. POSTERITY
   Future generations

4. LOLEGAICODI = 4. IDEOLOGICAL
   Having to do with the opinions of a person or political movement

5. DMEIIGNNP = 5. IMPENDING
   About to happen

6. DCEZUTISNRI = 6. SCRUTINIZED
   Examined carefully

7. LIOCIAGSHER = 7. OLIGARCHIES
   Governments ruled by only a few people

8. OTESAAGB = 8. SABOTAGE
   Damage or destruction done as an attack

9. YRIETNGTI = 9. INTEGRITY
   Honesty; sincerity

10. COINSERPI =10. PRECISION
    Accuracy; exactness

11. SORICEIF =11. ORIFICES
    Openings; holes

12. ATPAMISRGM =12. PRAGMATISM
    Judging things on their practical consequences

13. VUDETOCONL =13. CONVOLUTED
    Having folds or winding curves

14. XBYEANRLIO =14. INEXORABLY
    Relentlessly; unyielding

15. ACUELBPL =15. CULPABLE
    Deserving blame

1984 VOCABULARY JUGGLE LETTERS 3

1. YRUBDISAT = 1. _____
   Nonsense

2. GODATAIEDNR = 2. _____
   Worn or broken down condition

3. ELPLBAAP = 3. _____
   Easily seen or heard and recognized

4. DAUYSISIBR = 4. _____
   Secondary

5. BSYAS = 5. _____
   Lowest depth

6. YIOTRCTA = 6. _____
   Extreme wickedness or cruelty

7. ICIFAONTMSRIA = 7. _____
   Branches; subdivisions

8. EOVCITDNR = 8. _____
   Planned; designed

9. ROAJNG = 9. _____
   Language of a special group

10. PGERSU =10. _____
    Removal of undesirable people from a nation or party

11. LTLOBNEIRAE =11. _____
    Too much to be endured

12. UERICENSS =12. _____
    Very easy jobs that pay well

13. NRIIMTCNGINAI =13. _____
    Showing guilt

14. ITCREEAAD =14. _____
    Destroy; wipe out

15. PISRSOUU =15. _____
    False; not genuine

Copyrighted Materials

1984 VOCABULARY JUGGLE LETTERS 3 KEY

1. YRUBDISAT = 1. ABSURDITY
   Nonsense

2. GODATAIEDNR = 2. DEGRADATION
   Worn or broken down condition

3. ELPLBAAP = 3. PALPABLE
   Easily seen or heard and recognized

4. DAUYSISIBR = 4. SUBSIDIARY
   Secondary

5. BSYAS = 5. ABYSS
   Lowest depth

6. YIOTRCTA = 6. ATROCITY
   Extreme wickedness or cruelty

7. ICIFAONTMSRIA = 7. RAMIFICATIONS
   Branches; subdivisions

8. EOVCITDNR = 8. CONTRIVED
   Planned; designed

9. ROAJNG = 9. JARGON
   Language of a special group

10. PGERSU =10. PURGES
    Removal of undesirable people from a nation or party

11. LTLOBNEIRAE =11. INTOLERABLE
    Too much to be endured

12. UERICENSS =12. SINECURES
    Very easy jobs that pay well

13. NRIIMTCNGINAI =13. INCRIMINATING
    Showing guilt

14. ITCREEAAD =14. ERADICATE
    Destroy; wipe out

15. PISRSOUU =15. SPURIOUS
    False; not genuine

1984 VOCABULARY JUGGLE LETTERS 4

1. NIRGCMANIITIN = 1. _____
   Showing guilt

2. IMHPSEEUSM = 2. _____
   Mild or indirect expressions

3. GAOEDIRTDNA = 3. _____
   Worn or broken down condition

4. GATAEOSB = 4. _____
   Damage or destruction done as an attack

5. ELYUIDTOLSR = 5. _____
   Jumping from one topic to another

6. UAELCBLP = 6. _____
   Deserving blame

7. RTSDIBAYU = 7. _____
   Nonsense

8. IUIYQNTI = 8. _____
   Wickedness

9. NEGIYITTR = 9. _____
   Honesty; sincerity

10. NOCITOMMO = 10. _____
    Excited noise and activity

11. POUIUSRS = 11. _____
    False; not genuine

12. LCDAAMUEUCT = 12. _____
    Collected

13. SPAITLAISCT = 13. _____
    People who use money to carry on business

14. NADREEMO = 14. _____
    Behavior; manner

15. SPRIIEGOD = 15. _____
    Marvelous examples

ABASHED	Embarrassed
ABSURDITY	Nonsense
ABYSS	Lowest depth
ACCUMULATED	Collected
ARBITRARY	Without regard to a rule or law
ATROCITY	Extreme wickedness or cruelty

AXIOM	Statement taken to be true without proof
BIGOTED	Unreasonably attached to an opinion or belief
CALLOUSNESS	An unfeeling manner; hard-heartedness
CAPITALISTS	People who use money to carry on business
CAPITULATED	Gave up
CLANDESTINELY	Done in a secret or underhanded manner

COMMOTION	Excited noise and activity
CONSUMPTION	Things made to be used up
CONTRIVED	Planned; designed
CONVOLUTED	Having folds or winding curves
CULPABLE	Deserving blame
DEGRADATION	Worn or broken down condition

DEMEANOR	Behavior; manner
DESULTORILY	Jumping from one topic to another
DIMINUTION	Reduction; decrease
EMACIATION	Losing flesh; wasting away
EMPIRICAL	Based on experiment and observation
ENVELOPING	Surrounding

EQUIVOCATION	Not making a commitment on a matter
ERADICATE	Destroy; wipe out
EUPHEMISMS	Mild or indirect expressions
EUPHONY	Combination of pleasant sounds
EXTRICATE	Set free; release
FATUOUS	Silly; foolish

HIERARCHIAL	Arranging things one above the other by rank
IDEOLOGICAL	Having to do with the opinions of a person or political movement
IMPENDING	About to happen
IMPREGNABLE	Won't give in to force or persuasion
INCREDULITY	Lack of belief
INCREDULOUS	Not believing

INCRIMINATING	Showing guilt
INDIGNATION	Anger combined with disapproval
INDOCTRINATE	Teach a belief or principal
INEXORABLY	Relentlessly; unyielding
INFALLIBLE	Free from error
INIMICAL	Harmful; unfavorable

INIQUITY	Wickedness
INSTALLMENTS	Parts of a series
INTEGRITY	Honesty; sincerity
INTIMIDATING	Frightening
INTOLERABLE	Too much to be endured
INVIOLATE	Unbroken; uninjured

IRONICAL	Expressing one thing and meaning another
IRRECONCILABLE	Not able to agree
JARGON	Language of a special group
LETHARGY	Drowsy dullness or lack of activity
LUMINOUS	Shining by its own light
MALLEABLE	Able to be shaped or molded

METAPHYSICS	An attempt to explain reality and knowledge
OLIGARCHIES	Governments ruled by only a few people
OMNIPOTENT	Having great power or influence
ORIFICES	Openings; holes
PALPABLE	Easily seen or heard and recognized
PERCEPTIBLE	Observable; understandable

PERSIFLAGE	Joking talk or writing
POSTERITY	Future generations
PRAGMATISM	Judging things on their practical consequences
PRECISION	Accuracy; exactness
PRODIGIES	Marvelous examples
PROLETARIAT	The lowest economic or social class

PROSTRATED	Lying down flat
PURGES	Removal of undesirable people from a nation or party
RAMIFICATIONS	Branches; subdivisions
RASH	Hasty and careless
RECONCILIATION	Bringing together again in friendship
SABOTAGE	Damage or destruction done as an attack

SCRUTINIZED	Examined carefully
SERVILE	Giving in because of fear
SINECURES	Very easy jobs that pay well
SMUGLY	In a way that is too pleased with oneself
SOCIALISM	Government production and distribution of goods
SPURIOUS	False; not genuine

STRIDENT	Having a harsh sound
SUBSIDIARY	Secondary
SUCCUMBED	Gave way; yielded
SUPERFLUOUS	Unnecessary
TACITLY	Understood without being openly said
TORPID	Dull; inactive

UNDECIPHERABLE	Not clear
UNORTHODOXY	Not holding generally accepted beliefs
VAGUE	Not definite or precise
VINDICATE	Excuse; absolve
ZEALOT	Person who shows too much enthusiasm; a fanatic

1984 Vocabulary

CONTRIVED	PURGES	SINECURES	RAMIFICATIONS	EUPHEMISMS
OMNIPOTENT	INIMICAL	EQUIVOCATION	IRONICAL	SMUGLY
IRRECONCILABLE	MALLEABLE	FREE SPACE	PRODIGIES	UNDECIPHERABLE
INCREDULOUS	SCRUTINIZED	CLANDESTINELY	RECONCILIATION	ERADICATE
INVIOLATE	COMMOTION	IMPREGNABLE	IDEOLOGICAL	INDOCTRINATE

1984 Vocabulary

ATROCITY	INTIMIDATING	PRAGMATISM	DESULTORILY	TACITLY
SOCIALISM	CAPITULATED	ACCUMULATED	CAPITALISTS	ENVELOPING
SUBSIDIARY	EXTRICATE	FREE SPACE	PROSTRATED	ORIFICES
SUCCUMBED	SPURIOUS	METAPHYSICS	PERSIFLAGE	INIQUITY
INCREDULITY	STRIDENT	LETHARGY	ABASHED	INCRIMINATING

1984 Vocabulary

CONVOLUTED	SUCCUMBED	ACCUMULATED	PRECISION	INIQUITY
PRODIGIES	SERVILE	INEXORABLY	EQUIVOCATION	SOCIALISM
INFALLIBLE	INTIMIDATING	FREE SPACE	PERCEPTIBLE	IMPENDING
SUBSIDIARY	JARGON	CALLOUSNESS	ABASHED	IDEOLOGICAL
CONSUMPTION	LUMINOUS	COMMOTION	PERSIFLAGE	UNDECIPHERABLE

1984 Vocabulary

INTOLERABLE	PROLETARIAT	ARBITRARY	CAPITALISTS	INCREDULOUS
HIERARCHIAL	EXTRICATE	METAPHYSICS	ENVELOPING	INCRIMINATING
ABSURDITY	EMACIATION	FREE SPACE	SUPERFLUOUS	DEMEANOR
SINECURES	RECONCILIATION	ORIFICES	ZEALOT	PALPABLE
AXIOM	PURGES	INVIOLATE	EUPHONY	SPURIOUS

1984 Vocabulary

CAPITALISTS	VAGUE	SABOTAGE	SPURIOUS	SMUGLY
CALLOUSNESS	BIGOTED	DESULTORILY	INFALLIBLE	CULPABLE
PERCEPTIBLE	SUPERFLUOUS	FREE SPACE	PURGES	CONTRIVED
JARGON	ENVELOPING	RAMIFICATIONS	ABASHED	DIMINUTION
EMACIATION	SOCIALISM	METAPHYSICS	EQUIVOCATION	OMNIPOTENT

1984 Vocabulary

ATROCITY	STRIDENT	RECONCILIATION	PRAGMATISM	IDEOLOGICAL
TACITLY	INCREDULOUS	TORPID	INEXORABLY	LETHARGY
ZEALOT	IRONICAL	FREE SPACE	DEGRADATION	ABSURDITY
POSTERITY	CONVOLUTED	CLANDESTINELY	SUBSIDIARY	UNORTHODOXY
INCRIMINATING	INIMICAL	INVIOLATE	LUMINOUS	ARBITRARY

1984 Vocabulary

TORPID	IDEOLOGICAL	OMNIPOTENT	LUMINOUS	SUPERFLUOUS
PALPABLE	EMPIRICAL	IRONICAL	ORIFICES	PRAGMATISM
IMPREGNABLE	SPURIOUS	FREE SPACE	MALLEABLE	COMMOTION
PROSTRATED	INCRIMINATING	OLIGARCHIES	AXIOM	ABSURDITY
ABYSS	EUPHONY	ARBITRARY	INEXORABLY	INVIOLATE

1984 Vocabulary

ATROCITY	EUPHEMISMS	SOCIALISM	UNDECIPHERABLE	SINECURES
HIERARCHIAL	RECONCILIATION	VINDICATE	SERVILE	CALLOUSNESS
RAMIFICATIONS	PURGES	FREE SPACE	METAPHYSICS	INIQUITY
TACITLY	INCREDULOUS	CONTRIVED	ERADICATE	INTOLERABLE
IRRECONCILABLE	DESULTORILY	INCREDULITY	EMACIATION	PRECISION

1984 Vocabulary

PROSTRATED	LUMINOUS	PURGES	INTIMIDATING	PROLETARIAT
INIQUITY	CAPITULATED	BIGOTED	INIMICAL	EMACIATION
DIMINUTION	ABYSS	FREE SPACE	SINECURES	SCRUTINIZED
INDIGNATION	SABOTAGE	EUPHEMISMS	ABSURDITY	AXIOM
IMPENDING	SPURIOUS	IRONICAL	SMUGLY	PERSIFLAGE

1984 Vocabulary

RAMIFICATIONS	INFALLIBLE	UNORTHODOXY	EXTRICATE	PALPABLE
PRODIGIES	INCRIMINATING	MALLEABLE	INTOLERABLE	IRRECONCILABLE
CLANDESTINELY	INEXORABLY	FREE SPACE	ARBITRARY	CONSUMPTION
VINDICATE	INVIOLATE	IDEOLOGICAL	ZEALOT	VAGUE
PRECISION	CULPABLE	TACITLY	INDOCTRINATE	DESULTORILY

1984 Vocabulary

PRODIGIES	EUPHONY	SUCCUMBED	INFALLIBLE	POSTERITY
PROLETARIAT	INSTALLMENTS	OLIGARCHIES	CAPITALISTS	SCRUTINIZED
VINDICATE	SPURIOUS	FREE SPACE	LUMINOUS	INTIMIDATING
SABOTAGE	EMPIRICAL	CONSUMPTION	CAPITULATED	INEXORABLY
ORIFICES	OMNIPOTENT	IRONICAL	STRIDENT	SINECURES

1984 Vocabulary

ENVELOPING	CULPABLE	RASH	SERVILE	TORPID
ZEALOT	PRAGMATISM	PROSTRATED	RAMIFICATIONS	ACCUMULATED
PALPABLE	CALLOUSNESS	FREE SPACE	METAPHYSICS	PURGES
VAGUE	UNDECIPHERABLE	IDEOLOGICAL	SUPERFLUOUS	BIGOTED
INIQUITY	INIMICAL	ATROCITY	INVIOLATE	TACITLY

1984 Vocabulary

INIQUITY	METAPHYSICS	ARBITRARY	EMPIRICAL	JARGON
SUCCUMBED	EUPHONY	PERCEPTIBLE	EMACIATION	CULPABLE
CAPITULATED	INDIGNATION	FREE SPACE	MALLEABLE	INDOCTRINATE
IMPREGNABLE	DIMINUTION	INTEGRITY	SERVILE	INTIMIDATING
RECONCILIATION	IRRECONCILABLE	PALPABLE	SMUGLY	DEMEANOR

1984 Vocabulary

INVIOLATE	ZEALOT	PROLETARIAT	UNORTHODOXY	BIGOTED
TACITLY	INCREDULITY	STRIDENT	RAMIFICATIONS	FATUOUS
IMPENDING	OMNIPOTENT	FREE SPACE	OLIGARCHIES	EXTRICATE
HIERARCHIAL	INCREDULOUS	RASH	LETHARGY	SOCIALISM
INFALLIBLE	ERADICATE	ABSURDITY	COMMOTION	CLANDESTINELY

1984 Vocabulary

ERADICATE	DEMEANOR	CALLOUSNESS	ACCUMULATED	RECONCILIATION
INDOCTRINATE	EMPIRICAL	INTEGRITY	LETHARGY	SOCIALISM
STRIDENT	SINECURES	FREE SPACE	INFALLIBLE	PRECISION
ORIFICES	METAPHYSICS	PERSIFLAGE	CAPITALISTS	HIERARCHIAL
ABSURDITY	IRONICAL	BIGOTED	RAMIFICATIONS	INCRIMINATING

1984 Vocabulary

PRODIGIES	ARBITRARY	INIMICAL	INCREDULITY	JARGON
VAGUE	PALPABLE	PURGES	MALLEABLE	ABYSS
DIMINUTION	CONSUMPTION	FREE SPACE	CONVOLUTED	LUMINOUS
CULPABLE	EMACIATION	IMPREGNABLE	ATROCITY	FATUOUS
PROSTRATED	UNDECIPHERABLE	SABOTAGE	SMUGLY	SPURIOUS

1984 Vocabulary

RASH	IRONICAL	CONVOLUTED	COMMOTION	EXTRICATE
FATUOUS	ACCUMULATED	LUMINOUS	INTEGRITY	IMPENDING
POSTERITY	INCREDULOUS	FREE SPACE	SCRUTINIZED	CONSUMPTION
INEXORABLY	TORPID	INVIOLATE	PURGES	SUCCUMBED
UNORTHODOXY	INDOCTRINATE	ARBITRARY	IRRECONCILABLE	OMNIPOTENT

1984 Vocabulary

CONTRIVED	INFALLIBLE	CAPITALISTS	LETHARGY	INTIMIDATING
DEGRADATION	EMACIATION	VINDICATE	HIERARCHIAL	EUPHONY
ORIFICES	VAGUE	FREE SPACE	PRAGMATISM	PALPABLE
PRECISION	SMUGLY	EQUIVOCATION	STRIDENT	ABYSS
CLANDESTINELY	IMPREGNABLE	INIQUITY	UNDECIPHERABLE	SERVILE

1984 Vocabulary

UNORTHODOXY	PRECISION	UNDECIPHERABLE	IMPREGNABLE	INTOLERABLE
INVIOLATE	PROLETARIAT	JARGON	VINDICATE	CAPITALISTS
CULPABLE	PERSIFLAGE	FREE SPACE	IRRECONCILABLE	METAPHYSICS
SUBSIDIARY	DESULTORILY	PRODIGIES	SOCIALISM	ARBITRARY
ATROCITY	RECONCILIATION	SINECURES	SERVILE	RASH

1984 Vocabulary

POSTERITY	CONTRIVED	IMPENDING	INTIMIDATING	EMACIATION
EMPIRICAL	OLIGARCHIES	RAMIFICATIONS	ENVELOPING	VAGUE
DIMINUTION	IRONICAL	FREE SPACE	ERADICATE	SCRUTINIZED
TACITLY	ABASHED	INFALLIBLE	INCREDULITY	LETHARGY
STRIDENT	EUPHEMISMS	MALLEABLE	INDIGNATION	PALPABLE

1984 Vocabulary

STRIDENT	INCREDULOUS	PALPABLE	CLANDESTINELY	AXIOM
SCRUTINIZED	INTOLERABLE	ORIFICES	POSTERITY	SPURIOUS
RASH	PRODIGIES	FREE SPACE	DESULTORILY	OLIGARCHIES
CONVOLUTED	SUPERFLUOUS	IMPENDING	ACCUMULATED	DEGRADATION
EUPHEMISMS	VINDICATE	ABSURDITY	INCRIMINATING	SUCCUMBED

1984 Vocabulary

METAPHYSICS	TACITLY	ATROCITY	HIERARCHIAL	SUBSIDIARY
PERCEPTIBLE	EQUIVOCATION	PRECISION	MALLEABLE	IRONICAL
INEXORABLY	CONTRIVED	FREE SPACE	INDIGNATION	BIGOTED
INVIOLATE	CAPITALISTS	INCREDULITY	INSTALLMENTS	DIMINUTION
ABYSS	PURGES	UNDECIPHERABLE	SOCIALISM	OMNIPOTENT

1984 Vocabulary

SERVILE	SUBSIDIARY	ORIFICES	INCREDULOUS	SPURIOUS
EXTRICATE	SMUGLY	AXIOM	CAPITALISTS	BIGOTED
INIMICAL	INTEGRITY	FREE SPACE	IDEOLOGICAL	INSTALLMENTS
CONVOLUTED	TACITLY	ABSURDITY	PALPABLE	INEXORABLY
UNDECIPHERABLE	PROSTRATED	SUCCUMBED	SUPERFLUOUS	SINECURES

1984 Vocabulary

CAPITULATED	CONTRIVED	DEMEANOR	EUPHONY	ARBITRARY
INIQUITY	POSTERITY	IRONICAL	ACCUMULATED	INVIOLATE
INCRIMINATING	EQUIVOCATION	FREE SPACE	INTIMIDATING	CONSUMPTION
DESULTORILY	DIMINUTION	RASH	VINDICATE	INDIGNATION
TORPID	CULPABLE	PERSIFLAGE	DEGRADATION	SABOTAGE

1984 Vocabulary

COMMOTION	SUCCUMBED	SOCIALISM	EQUIVOCATION	PRECISION
SABOTAGE	PRODIGIES	INSTALLMENTS	DEGRADATION	TORPID
ZEALOT	EMPIRICAL	FREE SPACE	CONSUMPTION	ERADICATE
IMPREGNABLE	ATROCITY	ORIFICES	UNORTHODOXY	ENVELOPING
IDEOLOGICAL	INDIGNATION	DEMEANOR	INDOCTRINATE	STRIDENT

1984 Vocabulary

DIMINUTION	INCREDULOUS	PALPABLE	RAMIFICATIONS	EUPHONY
UNDECIPHERABLE	VINDICATE	PERCEPTIBLE	IMPENDING	INTOLERABLE
SUBSIDIARY	CALLOUSNESS	FREE SPACE	INCRIMINATING	CLANDESTINELY
TACITLY	SMUGLY	AXIOM	POSTERITY	INTEGRITY
INIQUITY	PURGES	SINECURES	RASH	CULPABLE

1984 Vocabulary

INCREDULITY	PRODIGIES	DEGRADATION	INDOCTRINATE	SOCIALISM
IRONICAL	OMNIPOTENT	PRAGMATISM	SUPERFLUOUS	IMPENDING
SCRUTINIZED	SMUGLY	FREE SPACE	PERCEPTIBLE	PRECISION
METAPHYSICS	CONVOLUTED	DESULTORILY	CLANDESTINELY	INTEGRITY
INFALLIBLE	INEXORABLY	TACITLY	TORPID	MALLEABLE

1984 Vocabulary

ACCUMULATED	IRRECONCILABLE	INTOLERABLE	JARGON	EXTRICATE
CAPITALISTS	ZEALOT	INTIMIDATING	EQUIVOCATION	INIQUITY
CALLOUSNESS	BIGOTED	FREE SPACE	CONTRIVED	POSTERITY
SUBSIDIARY	DEMEANOR	LUMINOUS	RAMIFICATIONS	FATUOUS
INCREDULOUS	CONSUMPTION	EMPIRICAL	CAPITULATED	VINDICATE

1984 Vocabulary

UNDECIPHERABLE	TACITLY	PRECISION	CONVOLUTED	ERADICATE
ABSURDITY	CAPITULATED	SCRUTINIZED	ZEALOT	EXTRICATE
UNORTHODOXY	IDEOLOGICAL	FREE SPACE	RASH	INFALLIBLE
CLANDESTINELY	INIMICAL	PROSTRATED	PERSIFLAGE	ACCUMULATED
PRAGMATISM	EUPHEMISMS	EQUIVOCATION	VAGUE	OLIGARCHIES

1984 Vocabulary

ARBITRARY	CULPABLE	FATUOUS	INTIMIDATING	DEMEANOR
IRRECONCILABLE	INDIGNATION	EMPIRICAL	POSTERITY	PERCEPTIBLE
MALLEABLE	EMACIATION	FREE SPACE	ORIFICES	SABOTAGE
SUPERFLUOUS	SERVILE	PROLETARIAT	SOCIALISM	TORPID
LETHARGY	COMMOTION	DEGRADATION	DESULTORILY	ABYSS

1984 Vocabulary

INFALLIBLE	EMACIATION	UNORTHODOXY	COMMOTION	CONVOLUTED
DIMINUTION	IRRECONCILABLE	BIGOTED	PROLETARIAT	VINDICATE
SUCCUMBED	EQUIVOCATION	FREE SPACE	INDIGNATION	SMUGLY
INTOLERABLE	IMPREGNABLE	PERCEPTIBLE	STRIDENT	LETHARGY
PURGES	POSTERITY	DESULTORILY	SCRUTINIZED	EXTRICATE

1984 Vocabulary

PRAGMATISM	INTEGRITY	TORPID	INEXORABLY	RECONCILIATION
ORIFICES	IDEOLOGICAL	ABYSS	ENVELOPING	ATROCITY
SERVILE	UNDECIPHERABLE	FREE SPACE	INCRIMINATING	INDOCTRINATE
CAPITULATED	ABSURDITY	PROSTRATED	SINECURES	RASH
IMPENDING	SPURIOUS	CONSUMPTION	PALPABLE	INTIMIDATING